Employee Assistance Programs in Managed Care

T0271681

Employee Assistance Programs in Managed Care

Norman Winegar, LCSW, CEAP

Routledge
Taylor & Francis Group
New York   London

First published by

Best Business Books®, an imprint of The Haworth Press, Inc., 10 Alice Street, Binghamton, NY 13904-1580.

This edition published 2012 by Routledge

Routledge   Routledge
Taylor & Francis Group   Taylor & Francis Group
711 Third Avenue   2 Park Square, Milton Park
New York, NY 10017   Abingdon, Oxon OX14 4RN

Cover design by Jennifer Gaska.

Library of Congress Cataloging-in-Publication Data

Winegar, Norman.
    Employee assistance programs in managed care / Norman Winegar.
        p. cm.
    Includes bibliographical references and index.
    ISBN 0-7890-0617-0 (alk. paper)—ISBN 0-7890-0618-9 (alk. paper).
    1. Managed care plans (Medical care) 2. Employee assistance programs. I. Title.

RA413 .W479 2002
362.1'04258—dc21
                                                            2002071260

CONTENTS

Acknowledgments

I acknowledge and thank the following individuals for their kind assistance in the development and preparation of this book and for all they have taught me concerning employee assistance programs: Margaret Ann Kellogg, Sharon Webber, Dr. John Bistline, Dr. Roderick Hafer, Carlton Weinstein, Chuck Sapp, Jim Printup, Dr. Jon Book, Dr. Charles R. Freed, Dr. Michael Forrester, Merrie Rennard, and Joyce Johnson.

I also wish to thank the following organizations for their cooperation and assistance: Magellan Behavioral Health, the Employee Assistance Professionals Association, and the National Health Care Anti-Fraud Association.

ABOUT THE AUTHOR

Norman Winegar, LCSW, CEAP, has over 23 years of experience in the EAP and behavioral health care fields, both as a practitioner and an administrator. He is the author of three previous books concerning the managed behavioral health care field. Currently Vice President of Clinical Services for Magellan Behavioral Health, Mr. Winegar directed CIGNA Behavioral Health's employee assistance program and has held a variety of positions in the managed care industry. A frequent trainer, he is a licensed employee assistance professional and a licensed alcohol and drug abuse counselor.

Mr. Winegar can be contacted at nwinegar@comcast.net.

Chapter 1

A Service for the
Twenty-First-Century Workplace

This morning Teresa awoke to discover that a personal crisis is about to complicate her life—one that will test this single mother's substantial problem-solving
skills and her resilient emotional resources. It involves all aspects of Teresa's life
that are important to her—family, job, finances, and self-esteem. It's an all too familiar crisis, but one that seems to escalate with each reoccurrence.

This time the crisis is especially anxiety provoking, for she fears that it will cost
her her job. Only two months ago, when the crisis last occurred, Teresa's supervisor called her into her office. The supervisor, Ms. Oliveras, said she really liked
Teresa and wanted to help but didn't know how, and besides it wasn't her job. Her
job was only to see that the office functions smoothly, the work gets done, and
customers get served. She said that Teresa wasn't helping and was in fact becoming a problem and a hindrance. Reliable attendance was what the company
demanded first and foremost. She warned Teresa not to let this problem cause
her to miss work again. She even wrote the warning down and handed a copy of
the note to Teresa.

Teresa's mind races. If she loses her job and misses even a single paycheck,
she will fail to meet her mortgage payment. She will surely lose her newly purchased home for which she has worked so hard and which means so much. Her
ex-husband's hateful prediction that she'd fall on her face if left on her own would
come true. And then what will happen to her two small children?

Teresa's crisis is a common one in America, for Teresa is a member of the sizable, ever-growing minority of employed parents, about
one in five, who is single and experiencing a child care crisis (Bond et
al., 1998, p. 30). Her child care arrangements have failed again, and
she is not sure how to find other responsible caregivers for her two
preschool-age children on such short notice. Without child care she
cannot go to work. Her only option may be to miss part or all of the
workday to resolve the problem, at least temporarily. For Teresa, as
with other American parents, disruption in child care services is a
common problem, happening, on average, about once every three
months (Bond et al., 1998, p. 51). For a single, working mother with

limited resources, however, this seemingly small crisis may well escalate into a major, destructive, life-changing event.

Dennis is leaving his primary care physician's (PCP) office again. This time his complaint was about his headaches, which are becoming increasingly worse. His doctor ordered some tests this time, and Dennis is thinking about having to explain to his boss that he'll need to take another morning off this Friday. He is not looking forward to that conversation.

This office visit with Dr. Jefferson was different from the others Dennis has had recently. The doctor seemed to take more time with him. He asked a lot of what Dennis thought were personal, not medical, questions. Dr. Jefferson seemed especially interested in how Dennis was taking the medications prescribed for him about six months ago for depression. He emphasized to Dennis that these medications had to be taken exactly as prescribed. Dennis told him that he'd never been very good at taking medicine, while wondering to himself what any of this had to do with his headaches.

Though he doesn't feel well enough, as his headache has returned, Dennis returns to work. He is a technician for a cable television company and, when he's feeling well, spends most of his time in the field installing new cable service and repairing problem equipment. Although he dreads it, he knows he needs to see his supervisor to turn in the excuse he received from Dr. Jefferson, and to tell him he'll need another morning off for the tests the doctor ordered. His relationship with his supervisor, Mr. Hardy, has not been good lately. He even thinks Mr. Hardy is a little afraid of him now, after the big argument they had two weeks ago. He believes Mr. Hardy is assigning too many of the difficult assignments to him instead of the newcomers, as it used to be. In fact, Dennis feels a lot of people at work who used to be his friends are now acting strangely toward him.

When Dennis finally arrives at Mr. Hardy's office, his boss seems particularly ill at ease. His supervisor tells Dennis that he's been dreading this discussion for months. He makes a quick call, and in from an adjacent office step the company's security guard and Mr. Jensen, the human resource manager who hired Dennis seven years ago. Mr. Hardy explains to Dennis that his employment is being terminated, effective immediately. He and Mr. Jensen explain that Dennis's attendance has faltered, the quality of his work has declined, and his temper and irritability have disrupted his co-workers and managers. They point out that he's been warned before about the need to change but has not done so. Everyone feels badly about this, but since the merger, the company can no longer tolerate people not functioning efficiently. They tell Dennis that he's had his chance, and the company cannot be responsible for resolving whatever problem he's having. After he signs some forms, the guard will escort him off the property. His belongings from his locker are already in a box in the adjoining office.

Dennis is stunned and bewildered. He does not seem to have the energy to get angry. He remembers some talks with the supervisor about his work, but he never thought he was in danger of losing his job. Then again, Dennis has felt unhappy a lot in the past couple of years and many things have seemed a little unreal.

Though often unrecognized by family, friends, co-workers, and professionals, Dennis's situation is common. One in five Americans experiences a substance abuse or mental health disorder over the course of a lifetime (Von Korff and Simon, 1996, p. 162). Dennis suffers from clinical depression, one of the nation's most common behavioral disorders, with an affliction rate of 6 to 8 percent of all primary care outpatients (U.S. Department of Health and Human Services [DHHS], 1993, p. 2).

About half of those who experience a behavioral disorder impacting their social and occupational functioning never seek any treatment (Narrow et al., 1993, p. 95), and Dennis receives care through his PCP, not a behavioral care specialist. Studies have shown that of the half who seek care for diagnosable behavioral conditions, about half receive treatment only from a general physician, and that as much as 70 percent of all psychotropic medications and 80 percent of antidepressants are prescribed by general physicians (Strosahl, 1994, p. 177). Unfortunately for Dennis, his depression has not responded to the particular treatment prescribed by his physician. His work has evidenced a pattern of deterioration for months, but workplace efforts to intervene have been unsuccessful. Now, in addition to his depressive disorder and somatic complaints, Dennis is confronted with numerous psychosocial stressors associated with his newfound status as unemployed. His tenuous relationship with his treatment provider, Dr. Jefferson, will be disrupted by his loss of employment. Dennis will join America's ranks of the uninsured. Untreated, his behavioral disorder will worsen, exacerbated by financial and family problems that develop as a consequence of losing his job.

Teresa and Dennis have something in common—both of their dilemmas could have been effectively addressed by an employee assistance program (EAP). An EAP could have assisted Teresa in finding reliable child care and helped Dennis to identify his depressive condition early in its progression and to obtain effective treatment before his job performance resulted in termination. Neither of their employers offered such a service, making them part of the estimated 58 percent of American businesses employing fifty or more workers who do not offer such a benefit to their workforces (Oss and Clary, 1998). Yet thousands of American employers do offer such services (see Table 1.1),

TABLE 1.1. National Prevalence of EAPs by Size of Work Site

Number of Employees	Number of Work Sites	Percent of Work Sites Offering EAPs	Percent of Employees with Access to EAPs
All work sites	162,800	32.9	55.3
Under 100	61,600	20.9	21.0
100-249	66,000	33.2	34.0
250-999	29,000	48.4	51.8
1,000 or more	6,200	76.1	82.3

Source: Adapted from Oss, M.E. and Clary, J. (1998). EAPs Are Evolving to Meet Changing Employer Needs. *Open Minds* 12(1), p. 5.

and their numbers are growing, representing one of the few expanding markets for early intervention counseling and consultation services.

Businesses offer EAPs, not for purely humanitarian reasons, but instead out of a recognition of the prevalence of psychosocial problems in society, as well as an awareness of their negative impact on employee productivity and employer health care costs. In the face of fierce competition in the global marketplace, many businesses have embraced EAPs as a tool to extend their competitive ability. The awareness that a counseling-oriented tool can help employers' bottom line by assisting workers to remain healthy and productive has been one of the least publicized changes in American business in the past decade. To thousands of workers aided by EAPs and those professionals and students in counseling fields, it may be one of the most significant changes.

Employers need to ensure early identification and effective treatment intervention for workers experiencing behavioral disorders for three reasons. First, behavioral disorders are very common, affecting about one in five Americans. Second, behavioral disorders create functional disabilities that impact both social and occupational functioning; this reduces worker productivity and indirectly creates higher social costs that are borne by employers in the form of taxes. Third, behavioral disorders can escalate, thereby increasing health care costs if left undetected and untreated in their earlier stages. Adopted from Von Korff and Simon (1996, p. 162), the three most prevalent psychological disorders among presenting primary care patients most likely to be members of the workforce are

- alcohol abuse,
- major depression, and
- generalized anxiety disorder.

BACKGROUND

It is useful to think of EAPs as products. They may be sold and delivered by a range of entities, from solo practitioners offering relatively modest counseling services to international behavioral care companies offering an entire EAP product line. In sharp contrast to managed behavioral care products, health maintenance organizations (HMOs), and other health care systems, EAPs are largely unregulated. Though their goals remain consistent, their functions, features, and forms continue to change according to the forces of the marketplace. No one standard model exists. In fact, EAP suppliers compete fiercely for the millions of dollars in EAP contracts awarded annually by private businesses and the federal government. Each supplier promotes the virtues and features of its own EAP products. We will later examine how EAPs are marketed, and throughout this book we will use this concept of the EAP as a product.

EAPs have an unlikely and uniquely American origin. Their development over the past century is a testimony to the changes in America's attitudes toward psychosocial problems. The origin of EAPs lies in the temperance movement of the late nineteenth and early twentieth centuries. These popular initiatives preached the evils of alcohol and the merits of change and redemption. Although they approached the enormous and complex social problem of alcohol abuse from a mainly moral perspective, these efforts brought the problem and its consequences to the nation's attention. Inspired by this, a handful of progressive American businesses responded by establishing fledgling counseling programs within their business operations. These services were closely allied with early occupational medicine physicians and were often housed in these settings. They were usually staffed by social workers, and by the 1920s, the most common environment for the professional practice of social work was occupational settings. Social work today continues be highly represented in EAP practice. The goal of these pre–Alcoholics Anonymous, occupationally based counseling services was primarily to assist alcohol abusers and their families in an era long before the development of the social services infrastructure we are accustomed to today.

Although the Great Depression of the 1930s diminished the number and impact of these early efforts to offer professional psychosocial assistance in the workplace, World War II, with its emphasis on maximum productivity and worker safety, helped resurrect early EAP efforts; again the focus was assisting problem drinkers. The emergence of the Alcoholics Anonymous self-help group in the 1930s demonstrated the growing awareness in American of the notion of problem drinking as a treatable, medical condition—not a purely moral problem. This illness had a new name: *alcoholism.* A new term emerged for the workplace-based programs to assist problem drinkers—occupational alcoholism programs (OAPs)—and this term persisted into the 1970s. Kaiser Shipbuilding, owned by industrialist Henry Kaiser who also pioneered one of America's first HMOs, was a World War II era business that sponsored such services. Other heavy manufacturers, including Kodak and Allis-Chambers, also sponsored early OAPs. When peace and prosperity returned in the 1950s, the business need for OAPs seemed to decline.

By the 1970s, Americans once again were focused on the impact on society of alcohol and drug abuse, now termed chemical dependency or substance abuse. Americans were also more aware and accepting of the notion of emotional or psychiatric disorders as illnesses. Treatment of these problems through newly developed psychotropic medications and through new counseling and psychotherapy approaches also gained acceptance. OAPs evolved into so-called "broad-brush" programs, or EAPs aimed at assisting employees, and their family members, who might be experiencing a *broad* range of problems that might impact worker productivity. Large commercial EAPs, selling services to multiple employers, emerged onto the business scene in the 1970s, led by Human Affairs International.

The managed care revolution that changed the behavioral care delivery system in the 1980s was the next driver of change in EAP products. This dynamic laid much of the foundation for EAP products at the beginning of the twenty-first century.

EAPs TODAY

How do we know an EAP when we see one today? What are its distinguishing features if it is indeed shaped by market forces in a managed-care-dominated environment? Two useful definitions help us answer this question.

The first definition is from one of the seminal figures in the EAP field, Dale Masi.* Masi offers a useful description of the essential components of EAPs in a paper prepared for the U.S. Center for Mental Health Services.

First she defines an EAP as a

> professional assessment, referral, and/or short-term counseling service offered to employees with alcohol, drug, or other mental health problems that may be affecting their jobs. Employees are either self-referred or referred by supervisors. EAP services . . . include managerial/supervisor consultations; supervisory and union steward trainings; employee orientations; childcare and eldercare referral services; critical incident stress debriefings; workplace violence prevention; and employee education. Eligible clients often include family members of employees, significant others, and retirees. (1998, p. 1)

Today's EAPs involve more than the services described in the previous definition. In fact, Masi describes sixteen elements of current EAP services.

1. *Policy statement.* This document describes the purpose of the program, its scope, mandate, and the roles of personnel involved in its functioning. Policy statements are vital documents, for they represent an organization's endorsement of the program. Without such a statement, EAP's role is unclear and its effectiveness within the workplace is hampered.

2. *Toll-free telephone access, twenty-four hours per day, seven days per week.* EAPs offer access to professional counselors, not nec-

---

*Dale Masi, DSW, is a professor at the University of Maryland at Baltimore's Graduate School of Social Work and a researcher of EAPs' effectiveness. At the University of Maryland she developed one of the few formal training programs in the EAP field. The Graduate School of Social Work offers a Master of Social Work degree with a specialization Certificate in EAP Studies.

essarily for "telecounseling," but for referrals and crisis intervention, if needed. Increasing numbers of EAP consumers have access to, and the ability to obtain referrals from, counselors via their EAP's Internet capabilities. They can also access community organizations, self-help groups, and screening tools using this and other information technology.

3. *Assessment and referral*. Without an accurate assessment, treatment services for psychosocial problems can be ineffective and inefficient. Assessments for problems of a clinical nature are best done in a face-to-face setting with a licensed professional and can usually be achieved in one or two visits. Many clinical concerns may be resolved in this environment, as clients sometimes expect advice, clarification, information, or validation, not the initiation of a course of psychotherapy. Assessment of nonclinical problems such as elder care or child care concerns lends itself more appropriately to telephonic assessment. The term *referral* in this context concerns the resources recommended by the EAP staff to the client for resolution of the identified problem. EAP companies contract with networks of professionals called affiliates, or providers in managed care terminology, who assess EAP clients in professional offices or clinics. Some EAPs offer face-to-face assessment and referral services at the work site if the employer so chooses.

4. *Short-term counseling*. Masi notes that some EAPs offer short-term counseling, focused on a central theme and lasting four to eight visits. She explains that with the advent of managed behavioral care, an EAP with eight counseling visits is sometimes more generous than the health plans provided by the employer. In this manner, some employers who desire aggressive case management in their medical and behavioral care benefits to manage costs may still provide an easily accessed, relatively generous short-term counseling benefit. By providing an EAP through a direct purchase from a supplier, these employers gain much greater control over the administration of counseling services than is available to them when purchasing counseling services for patients (employees and dependents) enrolled in HMOs or other managed care organizations (MCOs).

5. *Other client services*. In this grouping, Masi includes the nonclinical services directed toward clients that have become typical of EAPs. These include child care, elder care, legal information, consul-

tation, and referrals. This is an area of expansion for EAP services, as they could potentially offer an array of informational, or nonclinical, services to clients. Additional services could include financial counseling, consumer information, and relocation assistance.

6. *Clinical supervision.* Masi recommends adequate supervision of clinical cases but notes that this often does not occur in EAP practice.

7. *Employee orientation.* This refers to a formal mechanism, such as a meeting, used to brief employees about the EAP and its benefits. Confidentiality of its counseling components is stressed. Many employers who express disappointment concerning low utilization of their EAPs trace this problem to inadequate or inept employee orientation.

8. *Supervisor and union steward training.* This training involves instruction about the EAP's services and the supervisor's and union steward's roles in the process. Supervisors learn to identify employee workplace behaviors indicative of problems that can be resolved by EAP services. They also learn how to make mandatory referrals so that the EAP aids employees whose jobs are in jeopardy; about the scope and limitations of confidentiality; and how to use the EAP as a consultation tool in coping with such regulatory issues as referrals of troubled employees and workplace violence prevention. Union stewards are also oriented to the EAP, although they do not typically make mandatory referrals of employees. (Labor organizations themselves sometimes sponsor EAPs.)

9. *Employee education and outreach.* These programs represent the prevention aspect of EAPs. Through these efforts employers are able to offer health education, wellness, and illness prevention activities for their workforce. Another benefit of these programs is their promotional value. Posters, brochures, e-mail, and video are also used to achieve educational and promotional objectives.

10. *Legal consultation.* Masi notes that managers, supervisors, and business owners are increasingly affected by workplace statutes, regulations, and rulings. EAPs respond to these issues by offering informed consultation and support. Key laws or rulings that impact EAP practice include duty to warn (the *Tarasoff v. Regents of the University of California* ruling), Americans with Disabilities Act (1990), the Family and Medical Leave Act (1993), and the Omnibus Transportation Employee Testing Act (1991). EAPs do *not* provide legal advice to work organizations or managers, but rather consultation to managers concerning

referrals of employees affected by workplace legislation, regulation, and rulings.

11. *Staff.* EAPs are staffed by full- or part-time staff experienced in EAP practice and with backgrounds in social work, psychology, counseling, psychiatry, marriage and family therapy, or nursing. Much of the direct counseling service components of EAPs are delivered by affiliated providers who contract with EAP companies but are not employed as EAP staff. Internal EAP staff refers to employed clinicians who work full- or part-time at an employer's work site for the employer, delivering EAP services.

12. *Confidential record keeping.* Although concern and controversy over the confidentiality of sensitive medical information in our electronic, managed care environment have increased in recent years, confidentiality has always been a concern in the EAP field. Due to the EAP's sponsorship by and connection with the employer, suspicion about confidentiality of records has always been a valid concern of clients. Masi notes that federal law (42 CFR, Part 2) has been interpreted to provide limited protection to confidentiality of EAP records (see Chapter 4).

13. *Community resource referral network.* EAPs maintain databases of a range of referral resources. One substantial value EAPs hold for clients is the ability to research available resources in an expeditious manner and to make professional, effective referrals that address clients' needs.

14. *Critical incident stress debriefing (CISD) services.* CISD is a relatively new specialty area of counseling services that has been rapidly incorporated into the EAP milieu. Through CISD services, EAPs seek to assist work organizations by reducing the impact on the productivity of their workforce of robberies, assault, homicide, or other acts of workplace violence, as well as workplace accidents, suicides, natural deaths, and natural or manmade disasters. Rapid response tailored and tempered to each intervention is a hallmark of EAPs' use of CISD services. EAP customers such as banks and retail stores—the unfortunate targets of much robbery and its incumbent violence upon employees—are keenly sensitive to the value of EAPs' CISD services.

15. *Funding.* EAPs are funded by employers (or in some instance by labor organizations). The most common funding mechanism is the capitation method: EAP companies receive a monthly fee per em-

ployee for all the EAP services delivered regardless of the level of utilization. This is a risk-sharing arrangement, in that EAPs must calculate and include in their fees to customers the amount of financial risk they take to pay for the services offered to the work organization and its employees. Costs of EAPs vary according to the features purchased by employers; the size, location, nature, and distribution of the employers' workforces; the efficiency and profit margin of the EAPs' suppliers; and other factors. (In the author's experience, fees of $12 to $30 per employee per year are common.) Unlike managed behavioral care services, one of the most client-friendly aspects of EAPs is the absence of copayments, deductibles, and out-of-pocket expenses. The client has no claims to file and no bills to pay. This strategy of EAPs presenting no costs to clients who use their services is an important mechanism to facilitate easy access. EAP customers rate this as an increasingly beneficial aspect of their programs, in view of employee perceptions or actual experiences of restricted access to services in managed care programs.

16. *Evaluation.* Evaluation of EAP services allows employers to determine whether the program is meeting its service, quality, and cost-effectiveness objectives.

Another perspective on the definition and components of an EAP today is offered by the Employee Assistance Professionals Association (EAPA). Founded in 1971 in Los Angeles as the Association of Labor-Management Administrators and Consultants on Alcoholism (ALMACA) and headquartered today in Arlington, Virginia, EAPA is the oldest and largest professional organization in the EAP field, representing about 7,000 members, mostly in the United States and Canada. It publishes a bimonthly journal, the *EAPA Exchange.* Similar to many other associations, EAPA reflects and serves the interests of its members, who are largely active in EAP work. Since professionals in the EAP field are drawn from many educational and experiential backgrounds, it also attempts to validate employee assistance as a distinctive profession and to clarify the nature of that profession.

In a recent *EAPA Exchange* article, MacDonald (1998) discussed the association's views on the definition of ever-changing EAPs and the essential elements, or "core technology," associated with sound EAPs. This definition stated that an

> EAP is a worksite-based program designed to assist: (1) work organizations in addressing productivity issues, and (2) "employee clients" in identifying and resolving personal concerns, including but not limited to, health, marital, family, financial, alcohol, drug, legal, emotional, stress, or other personal issues that may affect job performance. (p. 14)

Coupled with this definition is a description of what is meant by "core technology":

> EAP core technology represents the essential components of the employee assistance (EA) profession. These components combine to create a unique approach to addressing work organization productivity issues and "employee client" personal concerns affecting job performance and ability to perform on the job. (p. 14)

Seven elements of this core technology are endorsed by the this professional association. First is consultation with and training of work organization leadership (managers, supervisors, union stewards) concerning troubled employees and workplace job performance. Included in this element is outreach or promotion of the availability of services to employees and family members. A second element of the core technology is confidential and timely problem identification and assessment for clients' personal concerns that may impact job performance. The third element is the use of constructive confrontation, motivation, and short-term intervention with employees, and the fourth element is referral of clients for subsequent services. The fifth and sixth elements are two separate components that address consultation services to organizations. First is to assist work organizations in establishing and maintaining effective relationships with treatment and other service providers. In this regard, EAP staff sometimes participate in employer purchasing decisions for managed behavioral care services. The second component relates to an advocacy role, whereby the EAP assists the work organization in promoting availability of and access to employee benefit programs and services, including access to health and behavioral health care treatment. The final element essential to EAPs, according to this rationale, is a func-

tion that identifies the effects of the EAP on the workplace organization and on individuals' job performance.

To summarize, this key point may be made about what defines and
constitutes an EAP: an EAP is a constellation of services (products)
valuable to a work organization that helps it to achieve important organizational goals (such as ensuring a productive workforce) through
serving its managers, its employees and their families, and the organization itself.

SUMMARY OF EAP DEPENDENT CARE SERVICES

EAPs frequently offer dependent care (or work life) services as op-
tional service packages. These services afford employees and family
members the opportunity to gain no-cost professional guidance, advice, and expert information concerning managing common problems encountered with child care and elder care needs. Stand-alone
companies that specialize in organizing and delivering such services
evolved in the 1990s and are sometimes referred to as "work life"
companies. Employers offer such services in the belief that, if left un-
addressed, such problems hinder worker productivity and can result
in absenteeism, tardiness, errors, and accidents. As resources for employee benefit programs have become scarcer, and as EAPs and work
life programs evolved, EAPs have largely incorporated many dependent care services and options as a part of their core technology
(Turner and Davis, 2000).

Variants of dependent care services are innumerable, a testimony
to the receptiveness of the marketplace and to EAP innovation. They
are too varied to be covered in these pages. This section instead describes common approaches to how an EAP delivers dependent care
services to clients.

Basic Services

When a participant calls a toll-free EAP line about child care or elder care concerns, the EAP counselor may do one or more of the following:

- Refer the caller to national, toll-free child care and elder care
  hotlines or research services through a national United Way
  agency directory.

- Access the Internet, and other resource search tools, to identify dependent care resources or referral services in the caller's location and then refer to those services.
- Refer the caller to an EAP practitioner who can help identify local resources and/or counsel the member for emotional or family problems that often accompany dependent care concerns.

Case Example

An employee in Texas whose elderly widowed father was living alone in Maine and experiencing declining health was referred to the EAP by his supervisor. The supervisor had recognized a pattern of distraction and declining performance. When confronted, the employee acknowledged his preoccupation with his father's well-being. The employee asked the EAP professional for help in assessing his father's needs and in obtaining services commensurate to the elderly man's needs while preserving as much of his independence as possible. The EAP clinician in the employee's city contacted an EAP professional near the father's rural Maine location. The second clinician provided names of convalescent facilities, and the employee ultimately placed his father in one of the recommended facilities. The employee reported at a follow-up visit that his work functioning had improved because he was no longer as worried about his father.

Many EAPs offer on-site wellness seminars on common dependent care topics such as identifying and selecting quality child care or identifying and determining the need for elder care.

Enhanced Services

Some EAP companies offer enhanced versions of the aforementioned services that include these features: increased access to specialized databases, a greater array and depth of services, increased reliance on specialized staff to service dependent care clients, and a higher degree of due diligence to ensure some level of quality control on the part of the service provider. For example, enhanced dependent care service packages included in some EAP products may provide a range of referral services, such as arranging placements in family child care or day care centers; performing nanny or au pair searches and screenings; providing options in before- and after-school care programs, private schools, and summer camps; as well as locating programs for handicapped children, senior housing complexes, and nursing homes or other specialized nursing care facilities. Such program options also offer contingency child care, adoption assistance, college admission research, and tuition assistance, grants, and scholarship research. Still other options include convenience or concierge services to assist consumers in, for example, obtaining tickets for entertainment or sporting events or arranging household maintenance, such as contacting plumbers or electricians, all with the objective of reducing workplace distraction while improving productivity and adding an attractive employee benefit.

Such enhanced dependent care services usually provide, through a variety of modalities and media, a wealth of information services aimed at helping to educate and empower EAP participants through a wide range of parent, senior, child, and work life information materials. Recognizing that today's work organizations employ a diverse workforce, such materials should include items designed to satisfy various learning styles, languages, cultures, lifestyles, and religious needs.

THE 1997 NATIONAL STUDY OF THE CHANGING WORKFORCE: IMPLICATIONS FOR EAPs

The Families and Work Institute is a nonprofit organization in New York that studies the changing American workplace, particularly the connections between work life and family life. Findings from the 1997 national study are of importance to employers, labor organizations, researchers, public policy makers, workers everywhere, and all those interested in EAPs. These findings provide powerful support for the provision of dependent care services through the proven workplace benefit program, the EAP.

The Study

The Families and Work Institute's National Study of the Changing Workforce (NSCW) was conducted between March and July 1997.* Some of its findings are comparable to a similar effort, the Quality of Employment Survey (QES), sponsored by the U.S. Department of Labor in 1977. Thus, we can view the changing patterns and attitudes in work life and family life over a generation. The first NSCW was conducted in 1992, and others are planned at five-year intervals.

---

*The next study in this series is planned for 2002.

The NSCW was conducted by Louis Harris and Associates via telephone using a computer-assisted telephone interviewing system. The sample was randomly generated. Eligibility was limited to those who worked at a paid job or operated an income-producing business, were at least eighteen years old, were in the civilian labor force, resided in the contiguous forty-eight states (sorry Alaska and Hawaii), and lived in a noninstitutional setting that had an operable telephone. Interviews were approximately forty minutes long, and multiple calls to each participant were made, if needed, to determine eligibility or to complete the interview. Participants were offered $20 for their time and cooperation. Over 19,000 calls resulted in a total sample of 2,877 wage and salaried American workers (Bond, Galinsky, and Swanberg, 1998, pp. 165-166).

Some adjustments to the sample size in the 1997 NSCW were made when comparing findings to the 1977 QES due to methodological differences. The minimum threshold for statistical significance in the NSCW findings is $p < .01$.* In its analysis to explain the variability or differences in job satisfaction, the NSCW used multiple linear regression analysis to evaluate the explanatory power of different sets of factors. The study defined employees as married both when they reported they were legally married and when they reported they were living together as partners. Employees were classified as parents if they had children residing with them or under their guardianship at least half of the time.

Key Findings from the 1997 Study

Demographics of the Workplace

Male: 53 percent
Female: 47 percent
Age (in 1997)
- Under 33: 31 percent
- 33 to 51: 54 percent
- 51 and older: 31 percent

---

*This means that a difference reported as significant would occur by random chance only 1 time in 100, and that 99 times out of 100 the finding reflects a real difference.

Education
  • High school or less: 36 percent
  • Some postsecondary: 33 percent
  • College degree or more: 31 percent
Race/ethnicity
  • White: 80 percent
  • African American: 12 percent
  • All others: 9 percent
Occupational category
  • Managerial/professional: 34 percent
  • All others: 66 percent

Family Life Facts

  • Eighty-five percent of employees lived in households with family members.
  • Sixty-five percent were married or partnered.
  • More than one-third (35 percent) had small children (under thirteen) requiring supervision during work hours.
  • Nineteen percent had children under six years old living at home.
  • Nearly half (46 percent) had children under eighteen at home during work hours.
  • More Americans than ever, almost one in five wage earners (19 percent), were raising children as single parents; 74 percent of these workers were women.
  • At least one in eight workers (13 percent) had a second, part-time job. The most common reason was to make ends meet financially.
  • Mothers continued to spend more time caring for and doing things with their children during workdays than did fathers— 3.2 versus 2.3 hours per day. This represented a narrowing of the gender gap in child-rearing activities in relation to the QES survey in 1977. While fathers had increased the time they spend with their children during the work week over the past generation, mothers' time with children had not changed significantly, even though mothers were more likely to be employed as wage earners. Mothers' preservation of time with their children despite workplace demands may be explained by

other facts revealed in the study. For example, compared to the previous generation, fathers spent more time doing household chores during workdays, up from 1.2 to 2.2 hours, while mothers' time spent on household chores decreased from 3.7 to 3.1 hours per workday. Despite this extra help around the home, mothers (and fathers alike) reported ($p < .0001$) having less time for personal activities.

- One-third of employees reported that within the past three months a family or personal life problem or concern had kept them from concentrating on the job. Almost the same number (28 percent), for the same period of time, reported that their family or personal life had drained them of the energy they needed for work.

Child and Elder Care Duties and Obligations

- Nearly half (47 percent) of employed parents, including those with partners who are not employed outside the home, depended on their spouses or partners for primary child care for very small children (defined as those children not yet in school). A slight majority counted on other resources for care and supervision of their preschoolers. One out of five depended on a child care center for such care, while the rest depended on relatives or nonrelatives.
- Twenty-nine percent of employed parents had to manage a child care services breakdown within the past three months. This crisis occurred when their regular resource was not available. The implication of this information for Employee Assistance Professionals and for managers and supervisors is that about every three months or so, employed parents were distracted from work due to the need to manage a child care services crisis.
- Child care is not the only concern of American workers. Many are confronted with the need to understand and utilize the complex and costly environment of elder care services. (The survey defined this as special attention or care for someone age sixty-five or older.) In fact, the study showed that one in four workers provided some type of assistance to an elderly family member in the past year.

- Of particular interest to employers was that more than one-third (37 percent) of these workers had to take time off work to manage tasks concerning their elderly relatives' care.
- Forty-two percent of America's aging workforce expected to have elder care responsibilities within the next five years.
- One in five employees with children also had elder care responsibilities within the past year. This is the so-called "sandwich generation" of workers.

Employer-Sponsored Benefits for Child and Elder Care Assistance

- Only 20 percent of wage earners had employers who offered assistance in finding child care.
- More employers (29 percent) offered a program that allowed employees to set aside pretax dollars from their wages to be used for health-care and child care-related expenses.
- One-fourth of workers responded that their employers offered programs providing assistance with elder care services.

Opinions About Their Jobs

- About one-third (31 percent) of workers reported that they had to bring work home regularly.
- Sixty-eight percent agreed with the statement that their job required them to work very fast; 88 percent agreed with the statement that they had to work very hard.
- A large majority agreed that their jobs afforded new learning opportunities and allowed them to be creative and to use their skills and abilities.
- A large majority of those surveyed also agreed that they had at least a fair chance for advancement at their jobs.
- Nearly four out of ten (39 percent) felt it wouldn't be easy to find other jobs with similar wages and benefits if they should lose their current positions.
- Nearly one-third (29 percent) were concerned that they were somewhat or very likely to lose their jobs in the next two years.
- Over one-third (37 percent) of the wage earners surveyed reported that it was very or somewhat likely that they would

make a genuine effort to find new jobs in the next year. This figure is unchanged from the QES survey in 1977.

Workers' Job Satisfaction and Commitment to Their Employers

- Ninety-one percent responded that they felt somewhat or very satisfied with their jobs—4 percent more than in the 1977 QES.
- Seventy-three percent reported that they were very or extremely loyal to their employers, a 5 percent increase from the 1977 QES.
- Ninety-one percent agreed that they are willing to work harder than is required to help their employers succeed.
- Workplace support (flexibility, supportive supervision, positive co-worker relations, a supportive workplace culture, equal opportunities) was considered most important for job satisfaction (37 percent).
- Job quality (autonomy, meaningful work, opportunities for learning, advancement, and security) was ranked second in regard to job satisfaction (32 percent).
- Job demands (3 percent) and earnings and benefits (2 percent) were least important in understanding differences in worker satisfaction.

Implications for Employee Assistance Professionals

These are only a few of the findings of this landmark study, which, unfortunately, did not assess employee access specifically to EAP services. EA professionals and those readers interested in similar programs and services nonetheless will find these highlights to have several implications. The design and service array of EAPs are the most apparent areas for review in light of the NSCW findings.

The survey documented the commonality of the working single parent, usually a woman; the substantial portion of the workforce who are parents of preschool children, with their special needs and requirements; and the commonplace nature of the double-income family and its need for reliable child care services. The NSCW also revealed that crises involving child care services distracted employed parents from work and caused their families extra worry, inconvenience, and possibly expense. To employers, such crises often mean absent workers, or less productive employees, resulting in direct and indirect extra costs. Yet, only one in five wage earners has an employer who offers assistance in finding child care (and even fewer employers provide on-site child care). Child care referral services are an inexpensive and time-saving tool to address this problem. EAP design must recognize this need and add such services to traditional programs.

However, child care is not the only concern of workers, nor the only opportunity for expansion of EAP services. Many more workers, as revealed by NSCW, need to utilize the complex and costly system (nonsystem) of elder care services. In fact, the study showed that one out of four workers provides some type of assistance to an elderly family member.

EAPs AND LEGAL SERVICES

Many EAPs at their customers' request, can offer assessment of and referral for a wide range of problems that impact workplace productivity, including legal problems. Legal issues or questions, and sometimes the financial complications resulting from them, can easily result in diminished productivity and lost time from work. The EAP can reduce this risk for customers by providing access to consultations with attorneys at no charge to employees or their household members.

Many EAP or Managed Behavioral Healthcare Organization (MBHO) companies offer legal assistance services to EAP consumers through contractual relationships with a specialty company that organizes networks of attorneys nationally or internationally. By calling the EAP, participants are able to access lawyers in their community whose area of practice matches their presenting legal question. Participants are eligible for a free one-half hour consultation. The goal of this consultation is to resolve the participant's question or to develop a plan of action if the client needs further services. Sometimes the attorney may recommend further professional legal services to EAP members. If attorney services are recommended after this initial consultation, EAP clients are usually eligible for a substantial discount off the normal hourly rate from affiliated attorneys.

What's Included?

The following are some legal matters commonly addressed by legal services available to EAP participants:

- Domestic/family law—divorce, child custody disputes, child support
- Civil law—warranty issues, neighbor disputes, lemon law issues
- Real estate law—rental agreements, landlord-tenant issues, sales or purchases
- Estate planning—wills, trusts, probate
- Other—business partnerships, minor criminal issues, contracts

What's Excluded?

In general excluded legal services involve the area of employment law, due to the dual nature of the EAP client/customer—the *individual* employee (family member) versus the *employer* who sponsors the program. Any legal information or advice given to an individual client concerning employment law issues can have potentially detrimental consequences for the employer. Understandably, employers are reluctant to fund services that might in some manner aid employees in bringing litigation, or in taking other action, against them.

Examples of excluded employment law issues are

- work site accidents or injuries;
- co-worker liability (assault or threats);
- employee benefits issues or disputes concerning the agents of company-sponsored benefits or services;
- pension, retirement, and early retirement matters;
- employer-based civil rights violations (workplace sexual harassment, etc.); and
- all other employer liability issues.

EAPS AND FINANCIAL SERVICES

EAPs frequently offer some array of financial counseling services for clients. These may be as simple as a referral to local debt-counseling and budget-planning organizations, which are found in most communities. At the other end of this service continuum are the constellation of services delivered by credentialed financial consultants offering expertise and advice on a range of issues, including legal advice about bankruptcy law.

The following are common financial counseling problem areas addressed by these services:

- Auto financing matters
- Consumer matters
- Housing
- Insurance
- Personal debt
- Retirement
- Estate planning
- College tuition funds

EAPs do much more than has been described in this chapter thus far. Their flexibility in meeting customers' and clients' needs is reflected in EAPs' provision of services at workplaces during times of crisis or as a part of the routine employment environment. The following section examines one aspect of this versatility.

THE EAP AS AN ON-SITE SUPERVISOR TRAINING AND EMPLOYEE EDUCATION TOOL

Proactive EAPs offer a variety of on-site training and educational programs in the work setting. These services are offered during lunch periods, before or after work hours, or during scheduled work hours. They are often one or two hours long and are facilitated by EAP professionals.

Providing such opportunities is not a purely altruistic act. In fact, employers who sponsor such EAP activities have straightforward and self-serving goals that also serve to aid workers on a personal level. The employer's goal for such educational events is similar to the overarching goal for an EAP itself: to assist employees in coping more effectively so as to ensure a more productive and properly trained workforce.

Common topics for such on-site EAP workshops and educational events focus on ameliorating or managing difficulties in four areas:

(1) intrapersonal distress, (2) interpersonal conflict, (3) substance abuse (while also addressing the associated management demands for maintenance of drug-free workplace environments), and (4) the negative psychosocial impacts of occupational and familial responsibilities. The following sixteen subjects are the most common problem areas covered by these programs.

1. *Stress management.* Every employee identifies with stress as a symptom of modern workplace and family life. Workshops on this theme can aid employees in coping with a range of problems. The nonthreatening title encourages participation.

2. *Balancing work and family.* This socially accessible, common EAP workshop focuses on how to balance multiple demands of family and the workplace.

3. *Coping with difficult people.* Employees frequently acknowledge knowing or having to work with difficult people, although they infrequently acknowledge considering themselves to be difficult. Employees learn that, although they can't change difficult people, they can change how they interact with them. Employees role-play and practice coping skills helpful in working with difficult people.

4. *Resolving workplace conflict.* This EAP workshop helps employees explore a variety of ways to view and understand the nature of conflict and how we react to it. Practical suggestions for resolving conflict are presented.

5. *Improving workplace communication.* This EAP program offers suggestions on how to develop an open, interpersonal style that can improve personal and professional relationships.

6. *Preventing workplace violence.* Although horrific stories of violence in the workplace have become commonplace news items, more common are incidents that are less dramatic but equally disruptive of the workplace. Organizations can use this EAP on-site program to encourage employee awareness of and to explore ways to prevent workplace violence.

7. *Managing people.* An EAP's workplace support services provide a valuable resource for managers whenever an employee's personal problems may be causing a decline in work performance. Supervisors at all levels learn a process of "constructive confrontation" to encourage a safe and productive work environment.

8. *Alcohol and drug awareness.* Our work and/or personal lives may be negatively affected by drug and alcohol abuse, creating enormous financial impacts for employers and suffering for employees and their families. Learning how to recognize signs and symptoms, knowing how to get help for ourselves or others, and realizing the complexity of the issue are all part of EAP workshops of this nature.

On request, EA professionals can add Department of Transportation (DOT)-specific training to the basic alcohol and drug awareness program; with this addition, the program may then meet standards for DOT substance abuse training. A "reasonable suspicion checklist" and a review of constructive confrontation help supervisors who must deal with declining work performance that may be due to alcohol or drug abuse.

9. *Drug-free workplace training.* EA professionals are aware that workers at all levels may be abusing alcohol and other drugs, and that most abusers are actively engaged in the workforce. Employees can learn about problems associated with alcohol, depressants, stimulants, narcotics, marijuana, inhalants, and hallucinogens, and about how to help friends, co-workers, and family members who may be abusing substances. Supervisors can get additional information on workplace support services, including how to use the EAP as a tool for maintaining a drug-free workplace.

10. *Supervisors and DOT regulations for safety-sensitive employees.* Participation in educational events of this nature can help employers meet DOT requirements that all employees receive training and written communication about alcohol and drug testing and the employer's substance abuse policies.

11. *Talking with your family about alcohol and drug abuse.* When it comes to drugs and alcohol, people usually have more questions than answers, yet the stigma associated with substance abuse often deters exploration and dialogue with informed professionals. Employees will usually want answers to these questions:

- What are the warning signs of an alcohol or drug problem?
- What are the dangers and risks if I do nothing?
- Am I helping or harming if I talk to my family member, friend, or co-worker about my concerns?

- What if I am worried about my teenager? Are there preventive steps a caring parent can take?
- How can I get further help in my community?

Employees who are concerned about their own alcohol or drug use may be more likely to attend a program of this nature, rather than one that implies an abuse problem exists.

12. *Change in today's society.* This on-site EAP program introduces the nature of change in today's society, including its organizational or workplace aspects. It helps people view change as both a challenge and an opportunity for personal and familial growth.

The four phases of change (denial, resistance, exploration, and commitment) are discussed in some detail during programs of this nature. The participants also learn change management strategies for what they can control.

13. *Help with downsizing.* Organizational change and downsizing have an impact on everyone involved—those who have been notified of job loss, survivors, and employees unsure of their status or anticipating job loss. Survivors learn to acknowledge losses, focus on the work to be done, and, if necessary, prepare to cope with their own future job loss.

14. *How to choose child care resources.* Choosing appropriate child care is a difficult challenge—one that often produces parental anxiety and distraction from work responsibilities. With good information and guidance, the process of locating and choosing quality child care can be managed more effectively.

15. *How to choose eldercare resources.* Similar in nature to the previous workshop, this focuses on assisting employees in managing the stress associated with selecting elder care services.

16. *Helping someone with depression.* Recent governmental reports and media coverage have helped educate employees about the prevalence of depression and its impact. This workshop can help employees suffering from a depressive disorder or, more likely, assist participants in helping others to get assistance.

Chapter 2

A Managed Care Primer

MANAGED CARE STRATEGIES

A general definition of an MCO (or simply managed care), which also encompasses the MBHO, is a system that coordinates, through the authority of a contractual agreement with an insurer or employer organization, the delivery of medically necessary clinical services while monitoring and improving their quality *and* decreasing or managing the rate of increase in costs of the health care delivered to a defined population of consumers. These ambitious goals are achieved through the use of one or more of several common industry strategies. The first involves the alignment of financial incentives for consumers with the financial goal of the MCO, which is to encourage efficiency in service provision.

MCOs and the employers who sponsor them may achieve this goal through the implementation of benefit plans that typically provide financial incentives for consumers, or patients, to utilize a selected panel, or network, of physicians, behavioral care professionals, dentists, or other professionals (commonly referred to as providers) or facilities, such as hospitals, clinics, and laboratories. To incur the least out-of-pocket expense, consumers must select providers from within the MCO's panel. If consumers choose providers outside this network, various financial penalties may apply, up to and including no payment coverage by the MCO. Unlike in traditional insurance plans, the consumer incentives in these systems are aligned with the goal of the MCO—use of the MCO's panel of effective, efficient providers whose service provision is monitored by the MCO's quality assurance procedures.

In turn, these professionals and organizations have negotiated discounted rates of reimbursement from the MCO in order to receive volumes of patients. This is a second common strategy used by MCOs to control health care costs. By discounting their fees, individual practitioners and provider groups are able to capture a greater share of patient services (business) within a particular market.

In practice, MCOs develop and administer a variety of rate schedules that are offered to providers. Individual providers are frequently at an enormous power disadvantage in their business interactions with a large MCO. They may have minimal opportunity to negotiate higher fees than are dictated in the MCO's schedule. To reject the offered discounted fee schedule may mean no contract will be offered by the MCO, thereby causing providers to lose their source of patient referrals and the subsequent revenue.

Professionals have countered this development with several strategies marked by financial risk-sharing arrangements. These include case rates in which they receive a fixed fee per case, regardless of the degree of services required. Another example is capitation reimbursement. In this system, an individual or organization receives a fixed monthly fee per MCO member in a given area regardless of whether services are provided.

Professionals have also responded to MCO discounted fees with another initiative, often in combination with the reimbursement mechanisms just mentioned: the formation of group practices. Group practices afford professionals a better platform from which to negotiate fees with MCOs. They also reduce operating expenses and administrative and marketing costs, while enabling practice managers to assess clinicians' practice patterns and to modify them, if needed, to optimize effectiveness and efficiency. They allow practitioners to better monitor their patients' satisfaction, utilization of service patterns, and treatment outcomes, again with aim of taking corrective action as needed to improve services. All these functions that are aided by the formation of group practices are hindered in solo or individual practice settings.

Discounted provider reimbursement rates set by MCOs vary according to numerous marketplace factors including the number of providers and facilities available, the number of specialty services or providers available (such as child psychiatrists or ambulatory detoxification services), and the geographical distribution of providers. In general, organizations or professionals who offer services that are particularly attractive to an MCO may be able to negotiate individualized reimbursement rates, or exceptions to the MCO's standard provider rates.

Another MCO strategy to coordinate care and manage costs requires members to select a PCP from its approved network of providers. In this strategy, the PCP provides most medical services to the patient, with virtually all services covered by the health plan. Out-of-pocket expenses borne by the patient are limited to small copayments. Patients do not have to submit claim forms in this system. The PCP also controls referrals to medical specialists, for diagnostic testing, and for inpatient care, all of which can be costly. This is the physician as gatekeeper strategy common in managed care.

Another strategy, utilization review (UR), is one of the most important tools employed in managed care. Through UR processes, MCO physicians, clinicians, and administrators determine whether proposed treatments or treatment plans are covered for reimbursement. Qualified services are those which are medically necessary and which are provided in the least restrictive treatment setting available. UR processes also enable the development of guidelines for treatment of covered conditions and for research treatment outcomes and feedback of information into the system.

Almost all MCOs expend extensive human and information system resources conducting UR activities. To some service providers, UR is the most onerous and intrusive aspect of managed care, adding extra time, paperwork, and costs to their practice. To further complicate matters, each MCO has evolved its own idiosyncratic methodology for conducting UR, which adds an extra burden on physicians, facilities, and other professionals who participate in multiple MCOs.

In addition to financial incentives to consumers, financial risk-sharing arrangements and discounted fee schedules with providers, PCP gatekeeping, and various UR processes, the managed care industry uses a range of exclusion strategies to deliver efficient, effective care while containing costs: exclusion of certain diagnostic groups (such as V code diagnoses), exclusion of certain treatments (such as marital therapy), exclusion of certain provider groups (such as marriage and family therapists or chiropractors), and exclusion of expensive medications from formulary options available to physicians.

Though its origins date back to the 1940s, managed care emerged as an important tool in American health care only in the 1980s, and largely as a response to the high medical care inflation of that era. By the late 1990s, it had supplanted the employer-funded health care system that developed after World War II. That system, commonly called indemnity, traditional, or conventional insurance, features employer purchases of health care benefit plans that afford wide coverage and maximum consumer choice. Employers may pay for the entire cost of the plan (possibly hundreds of dollars per covered employee, depending on a variety of factors) or, more likely, share the costs of the insurance coverage with the employee.

INDEMNITY INSURANCE PLANS

With indemnity insurance plans care is unmanaged and consumer choice is maximized. Consumers select which physician or provider to see and how often they access services. Patients and physicians determine the treatment plan. Quality of care is a matter between the consumer and medical provider. Oversight is largely left to the provider or facility. Patient satisfaction and treatment outcomes are not studied or reported to purchasers, and quality improvement initiatives are difficult to implement and unsystematic.

The indemnity insurance plan pays for medical services after the consumer meets a predefined spending cap, or deductible. After that limit is met, the insurance plan covers further costs. The consumer may also have to pay a predefined portion of these additional costs called a copayment. Common copayments are 20 percent of total charges after the deductible is met. Professionals and facilities are reimbursed after submitting a hard-copy or electronic claim (sometimes patients must submit the claim form) and are paid on a fee-for-service basis.

With little oversight, maximum consumer choice, increased access, increasingly costly and complex modern health care services, and the proliferation of health care providers, including behavioral health care professionals, indemnity plans had become a major cost driver in the health care system by the 1980s. The increased cost of offering such plans to employee populations was borne by businesses. Especially impacted were small businesses. Costs were passed along to consumers through higher payroll deductions for coverage and through higher copayments and deductibles. These insurance products rapidly declined in the 1990s, with enrollment of only 15 percent of all Americans covered by this type of health insurance by late in the decade. The decline of these costly insurance products and services helped create the current market for a wide variety of managed care programs.

KEY MANAGED CARE FUNCTIONS

EA professionals benefit from understanding key managed care functions and processes that are common in most managed behavioral care programs. One of these core functions particularly relevant to the office-based EA professional is the outpatient benefit authorization or precertification process. Understanding this process is relevant to the EA professional who has assessed a client and is preparing to refer the participant for behavioral care services. Information as to how MCO or MBHO care managers perform this precertification process is useful in two ways. First, it allows the EA professional to better structure client assessments so as to provide actionable information in an acceptable format to the MBHO care manager who will authorize benefit coverage for outpatient care (or inpatient services, if needed). Second, it empowers the EA professional to be a better advocate for the client. As an advocate, the EA professional must be able to educate the client as to how managed care benefits are authorized, and thus how subsequent treatment services will be covered within the context of the employer's health care plan. Furthermore, with this knowledge, the EA professional will be better able to advocate appropriately for EAP clients within managed care systems.

A sample summary of an outpatient review checklist appears at the end of this chapter. MBHO care managers collect this type of information when making initial or subsequent authorizations for outpatient benefit coverage. Such information is commonly collected from consumers but may also be collected from referring professionals, such as EAP counselors.

MBHO case managers and their physician advisors work with clients, patients, family members, and practitioners to ensure that patients receive the most effective treatment and return to normal workplace or academic functioning as soon as possible. A case manager in an MBHO setting refers to medical necessity criteria from the initial evaluation of an individual's needs throughout the course of treatment.

These criteria are developed by experts in the field and are based on reviews of the literature and on professional expertise as to which level of care is most appropriate for treatment as client's condition or status changes.

Appendix C presents one MBHO's medical necessity criteria. Most MBHOs make such criteria publicly available. They train both their staff and network practitioners in their use as a tool to place clients or patients in the most appropriate treatment setting. By familiarizing themselves with such criteria, EA professionals are better able to practice and serve their clients and customers.

Roles of MBHO Care Managers

- *Initial benefit authorization* of the medical necessity and appropriateness of treatment and placement in the least restrictive treatment setting
- *Concurrent review* of care for continued determinations of necessity, appropriateness, and effectiveness with acute inpatient treatment typically reviewed every day
- *Case management* to promote continuity of care as a case is progressively stepped down from an acute treatment setting to a less intensive/restrictive level of care
- *Discharge planning* and follow-up that focuses on a patient's posttreatment needs and reduces the likelihood of relapse and recidivism

---

SAMPLE OUTPATIENT PRECERTIFICATION

Review checklist and documentation guidelines for use by MCO care managers, outpatient practitioners (OPs), and intensive outpatient program (IOP) professional staff.
Advise consumer of the confidential nature of the call.

Consumer's Demographic Information

- Name of caller
- Caller's phone number
- Date and time of contact
- Care manager's name
- Source of call—OP, consumer, family member, hospital, hospital ER staff or physician, EA professional, other
- Consumer's name

(continued)

(continued)

- Consumer's age and date of birth
- Consumer's ID number
- Insured's name and ID number (if different from the consumer's)
- Insurance carrier
- Medicare/Medicaid status and relevant information, if appropriate
- Employer/occupation

Rate risk related to demographics: Low Moderate High

Age > 45 years old
Gender: male
Marital status: separated, divorced, or widowed
Employment: unemployed or retired
Living arrangements: lives alone

Consumer's Clinical Information

- Symptom checklist (at least one item endorsed): "What seems to be the problem?"
- Precipitating or proximal event: "What led up to this? What prompted you (or the consumer) to call us today?"

Rate risk related to current stressors: Low Moderate High

Recent, impending, or early life losses
Health problems
Symptoms: hopelessness, depression, insomnia

- Dangerousness: "Are you having any thoughts of harming yourself or someone else? Are you in any sort of physical danger?"

Rate risk related to dangerousness: Low Moderate High
(typically greater in spring and summer months)

Imminence: the potential for immediate action by the consumer (a specific, concrete plan; an intention to act on the plan; availability of means to enforce the plan)
Severity: the lethality potential, i.e, a combination of high-risk factors and the presence of a lethal plan (hanging, drowning, jumping, poisoning, firearms)
History of dangerousness: includes ideation, intent, behavior, and family history of suicide

If "yes" to dangerousness, then assess for severity and imminence; document specific plan and means. Advise the caller of duty to warn others of the threat of violence, when indicated.

- Previous attempts at self-harm?
- Self-injurious behavior?
- Acts of physical violence/homocidal tendencies?
- Historical and current activities?
- Functional impairment: "Are you able to take care of yourself?"

(continued)

(continued)

Rate risk related to functionality: Low   Moderate   High
(ability to adequately care for own physical needs)

- Support system—"Do you have family or friends who can help you? Are you employed?"

Explore current ability to perform work duties and the illness's impact on work responsibilities. If occupational impairment is evident or suggested, explore EAP involvement.

Rate risk related to support system: Low   Moderate   High

Lives alone
Retired or unemployed
Recent or impending loss (to include job loss, financial loss, relationship loss)

- Current substance use: "Are you now or have you in the past used any mood altering drug or alcohol?"

If "yes," document substance, amount, last use, and years used.

Rate risk related to substance use: Low   Moderate   High
(greater when under the influence; increases with
years of use)

Substance use leads to disinhibition (poor judgment, impulsivity, and reck-lessness)

- Medical problems/medications: "Do you have any major medical prob-lems or allergies to medications?" "Are you taking any medical or psychi-atric medications? Who is the PCP and/or treating physician?"

Rate risk related to medical condition: Low   Moderate   High

Chronic medical illness
Poor prognosis
Persistent pain

- Prior treatment services: "Have you had any treatment for behavioral health problems or substance abuse in the past year?"

If "yes," document when, where, with whom.

Rate risk related to treatment history: Low   Moderate   High

Inpatient services within past twelve months
Discharged within past month

Summary Risk Assessment: **Low   Moderate   High**

Authorization Information

- Consumer's practitioner preference: "Do you have a preference for your practitioner? For example, would you prefer to speak with a male or fe-male counselor? Would you prefer an office visit that is close to your home or close to your work?"

(continued)

(continued)

- Care manager actions to refer the consumer
- Level of care approved, i.e., traditional outpatient, IOP, etc.
- Medical necessity criteria that are met (detail required if other than traditional outpatient)
- Name of practitioner selected
- Authorization details (number of sessions, time frame)
- Date and time of determination/referral
- Date letters are sent to the consumer and practitioner detailing and documenting the benefit authorization

Document clinical supervision dates and supervisor, as appropriate.

Chapter 3

Professional Roles in EAPs

EAP activities cluster into two broad areas: (1) direct services to clients and their family members and (2) services to organizations and their members, such as supervisors and managers (see Table 3.1). Professionals engaged full-time in EA activities may focus on specific facets of either area. Some professionals may also be involved in the full-time administration of EA delivery systems. Most EA services, however, are delivered through companies that utilize large networks of contracted providers. These contracted professionals are not engaged exclusively in EA activities; they often provide numerous other counseling or therapy services.

EA practitioners working directly with clients and their family members provide services that include crisis intervention, assessment, referral, telephonic counseling and support, brief counseling, and follow-up or treatment monitoring.

Services to organizations include conducting supervisory training programs and various wellness or health education and health promotion activities; consultation to managers concerning the referral of troubled employees to the EAP, workplace-related regulations, the ongoing development of policies and procedures regarding the EAP or related functions or programs; and program evaluation. CISD may also be included as a service to assist organizations in minimizing the risk of disruption of operations due to workplace trauma. CISD also involves direct services to employees. These interventions are aimed at helping affected individuals cope with the traumatic event, but they also have as their goal the restoration of normal productivity to a workforce or work unit to minimize future disruption to the organization due to the traumatic event.

TABLE 3.1. Common Services Performed by EA Professionals

Services to Clients	Services to Organizations
Crisis intervention	Consultation to managers and supervisors
Assessment and referral	
Telephonic counseling and support	Training services
Brief counseling	Wellness, health promotion, and educational activities
Follow-up counseling and treatment monitoring	Policy consultation
	Program evaluation
	Critical incident stress debriefing

Some EAP activities are quite specialized and are not routinely provided by most counseling professionals. Few social workers, psychologists, or counselors offer such services as "consultation to managers concerning compliance with Department of Transportation regulations concerning safety-sensitive employees." Few practitioners are trained and experienced in CISD. Fewer still work in practice settings that easily facilitate the immediate responsiveness needed to provide services to organizations in times of workplace trauma. Need for such services often can be most economically addressed through EAP delivery systems that utilize specialists for these and other functions.

For example, an EAP company might contract with a professional skilled in CISD who is available to respond to organizational emergencies in a particular city within a matter of minutes. This practitioner may provide such specialized services to a potentially large number of customers and organizations and may affiliate with multiple EAP suppliers.

Another example of how EAPs employ specialist roles concerns the provision of consultation services to managers and supervisors. These services are commonly conducted telephonically by teams of specialists serving hundreds of customer organizations, which allows for specialization and concentration of these services among a relatively small number of professionals. Such a strategy also facilitates enhanced quality assurance oversight and customer service.

Other EAP services are more suitable for delivery by clinicians with broader, less specialized practices. Foremost is the EAP assessment and referral service. Although this service may be conducted telephonically (again by teams of specialists), often it is delivered in face-to-face counseling settings. EAPs have large networks of affiliated providers to deliver these services. Some employers purchase delivery systems from EAP companies that offer assessments both on-site in the workplace and in professionals' offices in the community.

Two distinctions differentiate EAP assessments from other assessments provided by many practitioners. The successful EA professional is mindful of these distinctions and is guided by them. The first is that EAP assessments always involve a focus on serving two clients: the individual client and the organizational client. The individual client may be seeking services voluntarily, as a self-referred client, or at the suggestion of a supervisor or manager, and in a situation involving some measure of job jeopardy. The organizational client, the employer, is the ultimate purchaser of the assessment and referral services. Employers have as their goal to assist employees to resolve problems before they result in diminished productivity, employee turnover, or the disruption of workplace safety. These sometimes conflicting goals involving two different clients can sometimes cause conflicts within EA counselors as well. Nonetheless, successful EA counselors not only are aware of this unique characteristic of EAPs but are able to balance these sometimes competing client objectives to maintain the integrity of EA assessment and referral functions.

The second distinct characteristic of EAP assessments is their broadly defined nature. In contrast to an assessment for a behavioral care referral from an MCO, EAP assessments are not focused solely upon the determination of the presence or absence of a diagnosable mental disorder, nor do they consider coverage by the MCO's benefits, before development of an initial treatment plan. EAP assessments aim to address whatever is troubling the client—whatever process or condition that may distract, disrupt, or interfere with an employee's performance in the workplace. While this may include behavioral disorders, many other issues that are not typically the focus of purely clinical assessments also come to the attention of EA professionals, such as child care, elder care, and financial and legal problems. Other issues may include interpersonal difficulties involving peers or supervisors, behavioral or medical health care concerns or treatments, or disability and return-to-work concerns. Presentations for assessments in EAP settings may also relate to a range of family members' problems, since EAP eligibility generally extends to household members.

An implication of such a broad, far-ranging scope of assessments is that the EAP is equipped to offer services or assistance for any outcome of the assessment. This broad range of services available to the EAP client creates another responsibility for the EA professional interested in providing excellent services to clients. The professional must be knowledgeable about a vast array of community resources. In addition, the professional must be aware of the specific services provided by each EAP network with which he or she is affiliated. For example, some EAPs offer financial consultation services for employees assessed as possibly benefitting from such interventions. In this case, the assessing professional might refer the client to this product of the EAP. The client then would be linked to further services from a financial professional who might provide additional services still within the EAP. Other EAPs do not offer such services. In this case, the assessing professional might facilitate referral to other resources outside his or her EAP. Knowledge of the total resources available within an EAP is an important prerequisite to effective EAP assessment services.

THE CERTIFIED EMPLOYEE ASSISTANCE PROFESSIONAL (CEAP) CREDENTIAL

Ultimately, the value of the CEAP, and any other credential indicative of educational attainment, advanced training, or specialized skill, is a function of the marketplace: Are employers willing to pay a higher wage for EA professionals who hold the CEAP credential? Are reimbursement agents such as MCOs willing to pay a higher fee schedule for services performed by professionals with this credential?

The answer to the second question is that MCOs' provider fee schedules are generally, though not universally, based on the type of professional license held, such as psychiatrist, psychologist, or clinical social worker, and not on certifications. Although the attainment of the CEAP credential alone does not ensure higher reimbursement, its achievement may prove valuable to professionals in other ways. The credential may make the licensed professional a more attractive candidate for acceptance into an MCO network, or it may even be a prerequisite for MCO credentialing as an EAP specialist within a broader behavioral care network. CEAPs in MCO networks may receive more referrals for EAP services than EA professionals without this credential. Finally, the experience of the author has been that some MCOs require the credential for a professional to be employed in higher-paying program positions.

Are employers of EA professionals willing to pay a higher salary for this credential? Apparently so, according to a 1998 salary survey conducted by the staff of the *Employee Assistance Program Management Letter.* This survey of employed EA professionals found that CEAPs earned an average salary of $47,745 in 1997, about 4 percent higher than the industry average of $45,903. This survey also found that additional licenses and credentials equate to higher wages for the EA professional. For example, licensed clinical social workers (LCSWs) holding the CEAP credential had salaries of over $51,000, roughly 12 percent higher than the industry average. CEAPs with additional certifications also reported higher than average wages.

Other factors may be responsible for these higher wages, thus clouding the extrinsic value of the credential. The survey found that respondents holding the CEAP credential had over eleven years of experience, whereas non-CEAP respondents had less than eight years of experience. This means that employers may value the additional experience, not necessarily the CEAP credential. The survey also concluded that these veteran CEAPs work harder for their salaries: 53 percent reported working forty-six or more hours per week, while only 43 percent of the junior, non-CEAP colleagues reported working that many hours in an average week.

DILEMMAS FACED BY THE EA PROFESSIONAL

As we have seen, one of the hallmarks of EAP is their emphasis on service to both employer, or organizational, and employee interests. These interests may often be in conflict, however, creating dilemmas for the EA professional.

An Example

An employee of a manufacturing company is referred to an EAP by his supervisor due to tardiness, a violation of company rules. The employee is not fully aware that this is actually a referral to the EAP.

In the supervisor's mind and documentation, the referral is part of a progressive disciplinary process, per company policy. This process may lead to the employee's termination from employment. The supervisor, unknown to the employee, has contacted the EAP company to help assess the employee's problem. The supervisor wants an EA professional to recommend a course of action to remediate the problem, to motivate the employee to follow the proposed treatment, and to monitor the employee's compliance.

The employee is directed to an off-site counselor who is affiliated with the employer's EAP network. The affiliate's reimbursement for the professional services ultimately is derived from the referring employer. The worker states he is there for his "session" because he has been told by his supervisor that something must be wrong with him. That "something" is causing his work difficulties, and the counselor is to help him find out what that something may be. He later reveals in confidence information about the reasons for his tardiness. The employee reports a pattern of excessive drinking, hangovers, and sickness that results in his tardiness and coming to work with alcohol still in his system from late-night and early morning drinking binges, on some occasions.

The counselor, functioning as an EA professional with this client, faces a stressful dilemma. The counselor is mindful of her obligation to serve both the interests of the employer and employee. The employee's interests may be best served by her keeping as much information as possible confidential and advocating for the client. In her mind, the client has transformed into a patient who needs extensive treatment, advocacy, and support in order to overcome a substance dependence problem. However, she is also aware of her obligation to the employer's interests, which may include her obtaining authorization from the employee for disclosure of information to the employer. Such a disclosure would detail the nature of the employee's substance dependence problem and its implications for lost productivity and accidents at the work site. The counselor feels conflicted about her responsibilities.

Later in the process, her conflict intensifies when she learns that the employee has little commitment to recovery. The employee, now involved in an arduous, costly course of treatment for substance dependence, is being "monitored" by the professional in her EAP role. He reveals in a follow-up visit his resentment about the employer's forcing him into treatment. He reveals that his compliance is aimed only at keeping his job, and he will participate in treatment only to ensure that goal. Once the employer's scrutiny (including the EAP monitoring by the counseling professional) subsides, he will return to doing as he wishes in his private life. The counselor now wonders if the employer is wasting health care resources in a futile attempt to rehabilitate this employee, who seems destined to return to his old pattern of drinking. At the end of the day, the counselor, accustomed to motivated, self-referred clients, feels conflicted, confused, and discouraged. Trained to be a helper and advocate, she now wonders whether her obligation to the employer has placed her in the uncomfortable role of watchdog.

Dysfunctional Altruism

The issue of exactly what role counseling professionals should play with their clients brings us to the other common difficulty practitioners experience in their EAP activities: dysfunctional altruism.

Virtually all people who become counseling professionals are motivated by their interest in serving others. This desirable and necessary personality trait also has the potential to make EAP counselors ineffective. Seeing people change their lives or overcome illnesses and playing some role in that change is tremendously exhilarating to those attracted to the helping professions. It motivates, encourages, and inspires them. This altruism, however, has a dysfunctional aspect as well—one that come into play when clients do not succeed. Especially prone to this pitfall are inexperienced counselors who may have inaccurate expectations of themselves, their skills, or the counseling process.

When counselors see clients fail, especially EAP clients who come to the counseling environment with many strengths and supports and much to lose from failure, their altruism may result in a sense of misguided omnipotence. They inaccurately believe that they must do more; they feel a pervasive and even distressing sense of responsibility for their clients. This can result in their becoming obsessive workaholics, which may have its own constellation of self-perpetuating intrinsic and extrinsic rewards. Of even more grave concern is that this behavior may lead to a lapse in judgment concerning professional boundaries, which in turn can lead to inappropriate or unethical behaviors on the part of counseling professionals, however well-intentioned. Both developments may engender personal and professional problems or sanctions for EAP counselors.

Since counselors often work autonomously, these problems may go unrecognized by colleagues who might otherwise intervene. Expecting to achieve consistently a self-defined level of success, and realizing only incomplete and partial iterations, EAP counselors operating in this framework sometimes spiral into depression, isolation, and further dysfunction.

Counselors, of course, are not the only ones susceptible to this process. Bento (1997) notes that organizations and EAPs themselves may take on this dynamic. Some employer organizations create unrealistically high expectations of their members, thereby generating excess stress for employees and a greater need for an effective EAP. Paradoxically, this very culture of exceptional demands and high expectations may defeat the establishment of an accessible, successful program that responds to the needs of employees. This pitfall may become apparent to those professionals charged with the administration of EAPs or those who are in liaison with the program's employer organization contacts and coordinators.

What are the implications of these common dilemmas encountered by EA counseling professionals? One is the need for awareness among EA professionals to assist management of these issues. The unique dual-client (the individual and the organization) nature of EAP activities deserves much attention and consideration from practitioners, so that awareness of this duality is ever present. This duality contrasts with other clinical work commonly performed by practitioners in their practices, and the ability to shift attitudes and approaches while providing services is key.

The destructiveness of dysfunctional altruism is not specific to the EA profession. It, too, merits increased awareness, attention, and discussion. It highlights one of the important themes developed in the EA field—that people are any organization's most important and vital resource—a truism that applies particularly to the counseling professions.

CLIENT ADVOCACY

One of the traditional overarching roles of EA professionals has been that of client advocacy. This advocacy role is more complex in today's managed care environment, but it continues to be relevant and vital. As the scope of this book does not permit an extensive discussion of this issue, the focus will be two selected areas frequently encountered by EA professionals practicing in managed care-dominated environments: (1) how EA professionals can best advocate for their clients to achieve full use of their managed care benefits, programs, and services, and (2) how EA professionals can effectively ad-

vocate for reasonable treatment plans for their clients when interacting with MCO case managers as gatekeepers.

EAP Clients and Managed Care

Many clients seen in EAP settings are likely to receive their health
care services, whether medical or behavioral, through managed care
delivery systems. Thus, EA professionals need to be equipped to advocate for their clients in the effective use of such employer-sponsored delivery systems. To fulfill this aspect of their advocacy role,
EA professionals must educate themselves and then transfer that
knowledge for use by their EAP clients.

This section provides the reader with key information that may be
transferred by EAP counselors to managed care clients to assist them
in utilizing their managed care benefits, programs, and services. The
first portion describes the new roles and responsibilities of the four
main participants in employer-sponsored managed care plans.

Role and Responsibilities

1. Member or employee:

   - Understand the services offered by the MCO
   - Become familiar with your PCP
   - Keep records concerning your care
   - Be aware of how your medical records are used by the MCO
     or other entities
   - Make use of available health promotion and wellness ser-
     vices and opportunities available through the MCO
   - Take responsibility for your overall health
   - Know where and when to turn for assistance if unhappy or
     dissatisfied with MCO services
   - Be responsible for payment of copayments and other out-of-
     pocket fees
   - Become an informed purchaser of health care plans when af-
     forded the opportunity by your employer to choose from dif-
     ferent options

2. Managed care organization:

- Offer easy access to high-quality care
- Provide clear information about medical and behavioral benefits, services, and coverage
- Provide information about the providers and facilities members may use
- Provide clear information about the financial obligations of members
- Offer accessible assistance to members with questions
- Provide prospective members with key information to help them make informed purchase decisions about health care
- Offer an easy mechanism for members to complain, file grievances, or otherwise express dissatisfaction with authorizations, denials, charges, services, or providers
- Strive constantly to improve quality and lower costs

3. Primary care physician:

- Maintain a high level of quality regardless of financial incentives
- Coordinate patients' care to ensure quality and efficiency
- Become familiar with patients' medical histories
- Refer patients to specialists, including behavioral care specialists, appropriately regardless of financial incentives
- Ensure the maximum extent of privacy for patients' medical records
- Maintain satisfactory access to services and a professional practice setting for patient care

4. Employer:

- Offer employees health care coverage sponsored by the employer, if possible
- Offer employees as much choice in health care plans as possible
- Provide employees with information on how to select and understand their choices in health care options
- Offer cost-effective, high-quality health care plans

- Give ongoing feedback to MCOs concerning services to employees
- Ensure other employer-sponsored programs, such as the EAP, are integrated into the overall delivery system

Understanding Coverage

Many EAP clients do not understand MCO coverage, and EA professionals must be able to assist members in determining what's covered and what's excluded in MCO benefit packages. Today these packages often cover programs and professional services once excluded by traditional indemnity insurance plans, and they increasingly offer alternatives to traditional medical interventions. At the same time, they may have numerous exclusions. Remembering that no two MCOs are exactly alike, here are some concise tips for helping managed care members understand coverage issues:

1. What's usually covered:

- Any service authorized by the PCP
- Routine medical checkups or preventative checkups
- Hospital care deemed medically necessary by the PCP or specialist
- Prescriptions
- Prenatal and well-baby checkups
- Tests and diagnostic procedures ordered by PCP
- Services of medical specialists, when referred by the PCP
- Emergency room services for conditions that a prudent layperson judges to be an emergency
- Behavioral care assessment, counseling, and therapy services must know whether the PCP or other professional is the gatekeeper who must make the referral to a behavioral care specialist

2. What's usually not covered:

- Experimental procedures or services, except in extraordinary circumstances
- Most services not preapproved by PCP or other MCO gatekeeper

- Certain medications not included in the MCO's formulary of approved medicines available to members through prescription by physicians

3. Nontraditional services that some MCOs offer or cover:

- Smoking cessation programs, classes, and support groups
- Stress management classes
- Prenatal care classes
- Nutritional classes
- Acupuncture
- Chiropractic services
- Midwifery services

Managing the Managed Care Processes

For patients to obtain maximum benefit from services in managed care systems, they must effectively manage processes that are often new to them, and sometimes new to EA professionals. This task is further complicated by the lack of uniformity of procedures among MCOs and the fluidity of MCO populations. An employee may join one health plan this year and change to another next year, encountering processes and procedures that may vary tremendously. The most important is the authorization process.

Here are guidelines EA professionals may use in educating managed care members about MCO procedures involved in obtaining health care services.

1. How to get services authorized:

- Understand the dual goals of authorization: to manage costs and to ensure the clinical need for care.
- The PCP authorizes most care in most managed care systems. Make sure your PCP understands your health care needs and that you have a strong relationship with your PCP and his or her office staff.
- Ask how long before an authorization is effective. Some authorizations are not immediately effective, so services may not be covered.

- Use the MCO's member services department to resolve problems getting authorizations or questions concerning them.
- You may appeal most decisions that are made about your personal health care or your benefits. This can be initiated through the MCO's member services department or through an appeal.
- File a grievance or formal complaint with the MCO when you and/or your PCP believes that needed services have been denied or an appeal that is well-founded has been turned down. Grievances may be filed verbally or in writing, and they carry mandatory response times.
- Ask that your grievance be expedited if it concerns an urgent or emergency health matter.

2. Other processes:

- You can change PCPs. The MCO is obligated to assist members in this process.
- The MCO's member services department should resolve most problems concerning billing, claims, or charges.
- Always note the name of MCO staff who assist you and keep records of your interactions with the MCO.

EAP Clients and Managed Behavioral Care Referrals

How can EA professionals effectively advocate for clients when interacting with MCO gatekeepers? Clearly, this is an opportunity for collaboration or conflict. If this interaction becomes conflictual, the EA client may be intentionally or inadvertently drawn into the dispute over treatment plans. Drawing clients into these conflicts is usually inappropriate, and seldom in the client's therapeutic best interest. EAPs offer professionals incentives to ensure their advocacy is effective and appropriate.

This section discusses and illustrates effective advocacy using the example of the referral of substance use-disordered clients to outpatient treatment resources. Methods recommended apply as well to the referral of mental health clients.

Substance use referrals are selected as an illustration for two reasons. First, the treatment of substance abuse patients often involves the allocation of greater financial resources than that for typical mental health outpatients. Medical stabilization, ambulatory or inpatient detoxification, and intensive treatment services must be considered for substance-dependent patients. The potential for relapse and recidivism creates the possibility of further costly treatment in the future. For these financial and clinical reasons, such referrals may be given greater scrutiny by MCO case managers to ensure that resources are expended according to need and necessity.

Second, EA professionals often come into contact with these clients through referrals from supervisors due to the clients' deteriorating job performance. In such cases, clients' jobs may be in jeopardy and, therefore, these are significant crises in the clients' lives. Mindful of the client organization's goals, EA professionals have a responsibility to ensure that employees receive effective treatment and return to the workplace as productive, safe employees. Aware of their obligation to the individual employees, EA professionals have a similar duty to advocate for the best treatment plan for each individual client because the clients face important decisions about their health care that may impact their employment status.

Transitioning Services from an EAP Setting to a Substance Abuse Intensive Outpatient Program (SAIOP): Suggestions for Advocacy

EA professionals in various settings and under a range of circumstances often assess employees for possible substance use disorders. They frequently make treatment recommendations to the client, MCO case managers, and other behavioral care professionals based on the treatment needs revealed during the assessment. These recommendations often involve referral to an SAIOP. Here are some suggestions to aid the EA professional in communicating these referral recommendations.* They focus on the goals of maintaining a collaborative professional relationship with MCO staff or other behavioral care professionals and facilitating support and encouragement for the troubled employee to pursue recovery through the recommended treatment plan.

---

*These suggestions were adapted from Transitioning Members in a Managed Care Setting (unpublished manuscript) by John L. Bistline, EdD, LCP.

Assumptions. These suggestions presume that the client (or client and family) has been carefully and thoroughly assessed by the EA professional. They presume that the client has provided informed consent for disclosures of confidential information and that the current treatment provider or counseling professional, if any, has been consulted in the course of the assessment. They presume that the EA professional has concluded that the client is experiencing a substance use dependence disorder according to the criteria of the *Diagnostic and Statistical Manual of Mental Disorders,* Fourth Edition (American Psychiatric Association, 1994). The assessing EA professional has also thoroughly assessed the need for medically supervised detoxification. In conducting this facet of the assessment, the EA professional is assumed to have consulted appropriate medical staff and medical resources, if necessary, in conducting the assessment. The client is assumed to be stable from a medical perspective. The EA professional then is prepared to recommend a referral to an intensive outpatient program (IOP) of substance abuse treatment services.

Interaction with MCO case managers and treatment professionals. When discussing the referral recommendation with an MCO case manager concerning a benefit authorization to cover the client's treatment services, or a treatment provider who accepts the referral, the EA professional should consider the following points. Be prepared to support them with objective, clinical assessment information.

1. Explain why you are recommending an SAIOP service array (as opposed to a less intensive or more intensive treatment plan).

2. Stay focused on your advocacy goals. Advocacy goals include providing the right care in the least restrictive treatment setting, ensuring the client receives the treatment that has proven to be the most effective for this disorder, etc. Join with the treatment professional or MCO case manager around these goals. They should have similar goals for the client, although interpretation of the appropriate treatment, treatment setting, or particular facility, program, or provider may differ from case manager to case manager or from one MCO to another.

3. If the other party disagrees with your recommendation, allow the other party to save face (e.g., "you have tried or recommended one approach, but it may not be the most effective approach for my EA client"). Remain factual, objective, and unemotional.

4. Ask for a commitment from the other party to help you with this referral. Especially ask for the case manager's assistance in explaining to your client the referral rationale being proposed as an alternative to your assessment recommendations. Be explicit with the MCO case manager as to how the treatment plan recommendation is in the client's best interest. Ask for assistance with this individual client and work to prevent any triangulation so as to ensure that the client fully complies with the treatment plan recommendations the MCO is willing to authorize.

5. Before making any referrals, do your homework. Become knowledgeable about local treatment resources and all the relevant employer-sponsored MCO network resources. Make efforts always to suggest, recommend, and utilize MCO in-network resources for EA clients with MCO managed benefits. Advocate for inclusion of treatment resources in employer-sponsored MCO networks well before the initiation of any particular case referral. If, as an EA professional, you wish to recommend a particular individual or facility provider be included in an MCO network that you utilize, make this recommendation prior to case referrals. Understand the MCO's rationale for its selection of treatment providers. Avoid mixing the individual case with MCO network inclusiveness issues or controversies.

6. Sometimes an MCO case manager may not only reject your referral recommendation but also state that the EA client does not require services, or that the MCO benefits do not cover services which are appropriate and necessary. The MCO case manager may, in effect, offer no reasonable alternative treatment plan to your recommendations for your EA client. In this situation, an appeal or complaint process may be in order, although it may need to be initiated by the client. Be knowledgeable about the MCO's appeal and denial policies. If the MCO case manager refuses to support your recommendation for an SAIOP course of treatment, confer with a colleague or supervisor before initiating the next step in your client advocacy role.

Clients and current therapists. Sometimes substance-abusing, troubled employees are already engaged in some level of treatment or counseling activity with another behavioral care professional when referred to an EA professional for treatment of substance use. Common examples include employees engaged in marital or couples therapy, family therapy, or individual therapy. In such a case, be sure, with the client's consent, to involve the therapist in the assessment and in making other treatment recommendations; enlist the therapist's support. When discussing the need for intensive substance abuse treatment with such a client (and the client's family) or the current treatment provider, consider these points.

1. If the client already has a therapist or is in counseling for other concerns, first and foremost help the client understand the EAP and your role as an EA professional. Assist the client in understanding that you are making a treatment recommendation that is based on new information not available to his or her current therapist. Explain the rationale for the treatment recommendation and note the collaboration with the current service provider (e.g., "After talking with your therapist, we have identified another effective approach to help you with your needs or goals").

2. When counseling with the client, stay focused on your goals for the discussion, the client's goals or solutions, and the reasons you are advocating for this treatment plan. Seek to identify any of the client's unspoken, implicit, or underlying concerns to help address any reluctance (e.g., "I am scared to try something new"; "I think you are wrong that my abusive drinking or drug use is my problem"; "I really like my therapist and therapy"). Think through how to explain that participation in the SAIOP you are recommending addresses the patient's underlying needs, so that your goals, the employer's goals, and the client's goals become aligned.

3. Explain why this treatment approach is the best way to help the EA client and how you and the EAP will support the client and his or her treatment. Remember, even if the client does not like a decision, he or she is more likely to accept it if the client views the decision as fair and based on some objective standard. Explain how these programs have helped others with similar problems. Be careful not to discount or minimize the client's concerns (e.g., "You have every right to wonder if this treatment is right for you"; "Let me explain how I determined that this course of action is best for you right now"; "In our experience and research we have found this approach to be the most effective way to help people with your concern"; "Our professional practice guidelines recommend this as the preferred type of treatment in your particular circumstances").

4. Don't overpromise. Don't underdeliver.

5. Be aware of the power of influence, particularly concerning what is called social proof. Social proof is anecdotal information used to support or validate a desire, belief, or opinion. Examples include statements such as "My uncle got better without help" or "My doctor thinks all my trouble at work is caused by depression." When dealing with social proof, acknowledge the client's belief as a possibility. Explain the rationale of how you came to this determination, taking care to explain the fairness and objectivity of the decision (e.g., Some people are able to stop drinking or drugging strictly on their own, but research and experience show that the chances of successfully stopping are much greater for people who are in a specialized treatment program, such as an SAIOP, with support and assistance to make the challenging process of recovery much easier). Note to the client that an SAIOP is now considered the best treatment approach (a medical analogy may help). Indicate that you will want feedback from the client as to how he or she is progressing in the SAIOP and his or her opinion of the program.

6. Employ the "feel, felt, and found" technique. People, whether clients or treatment professionals, usually respond best when they feel they are heard and understood. This technique is a generic, yet helpful way of responding that is based on this truism of human behavior. By first acknowledging the client's concerns, confrontational interaction is usually reduced, while building commitment. Here is an example: "I understand how you *feel*. Many other people I have talked with have *felt* the same way. However, we have always *found* . . ." Phrased another way: "I understand how this may be difficult for you, and asking you to try something new, something challenging, may *feel* uncomfortable to you. When I have talked with others in similar situations, they *felt* just like you. However, we *found* that over time, as people gave this approach a try, they became more comfortable, felt better, and have often told us it was a turning point in their lives."

7. Give your EA client choices. Empower the client with the decision and responsibility for the choice made. Remember that clients have the options to refuse or reject professional recommendations and to ask for another opinion. Help the client understand the benefits and risks of all options, as they may pertain to both treatment and employment. Remember that a referral to the EAP often represents a crisis in the client's life. Your support and clarification of all the client's available choices in the time of crisis is an important contribution.

Chapter 4

Legal and Ethical Considerations for EA Professionals

INTRODUCTION

This chapter addresses two related and important aspects of the EAP field: (1) approaches to the delivery of services to individuals and organizations that have legal implications for all behavioral health care practitioners, including special legal issues of significance to the EA practitioner, and (2) ethical concerns and problems that are common in EAP practice and administration. Far from being an inclusive discussion of these topics, this section serves as a guide to the reader, steering interested parties toward a closer examination of relevant issues, trends, and development in the field.

ETHICAL ISSUES

Ethical standards focus on human behaviors and motivations that aim at the highest ideals of human interaction. In contrast, other codes of conduct, such as criminal law, proscribe certain activities in order to preserve the public welfare. Behaviors that violate ethical standards may result in professional censure, embarrassment, or criticism, while violations of criminal codes may result in societally endorsed punishments, such as imprisonment.

Over the course of the past 100 years, various counseling professions have emerged, and with them have come professional codes of ethical conduct. Such codes have effectively become one of the distinguishing aspects of professions, namely, that consumers of professional services can expect certain exemplary sets of behaviors in the interactions between themselves and practitioners.

These codes are based on the premise that professionals hold a judiciary or special responsibility for their clients due to the unique nature of helping relationships. The codes combine both high-minded ethical principles, such as the general proscription against abandonment of a client in need of services, as well as elements of criminal law, such as the mandate for reporting child abuse or neglect.

A psychologist is employed by a large practice association that offers EAP services to local employers and labor organizations. Employed as a clinician, she provides both direct counseling services to employees and training and consultation services to managers and supervisors. She is not involved with the business operations of the practice. To expand the practice and presumably enhance the employees' compensation, an advertising and marketing consultant is hired by the practice's director. The director and the consultant develop a marketing plan that includes a direct mailing to members of the local chamber of commerce. The EAP and other services are highlighted in the mailing. One statement in the mailing touts the EAP's ability to save the employer or labor organization "five dollars for every one dollar spent on the program."

As the individual providing the majority of the EAP services, the psychologist is troubled by this statement. The professional is aware that the practice has never conducted cost offset studies (due to their expense) and therefore has no documentation to support such compelling claims about the group's EAP. She believes the statement is not based on documentable facts yet is directly related to her own practice. She is aware that her profession's code of ethics holds her responsible for not knowingly making misleading advertising statements about her practice, skills, and expertise. She also believes that she has some obligation to correct others' misleading statements about her practice and is unsure what to do.

How can the practitioner resolve this dilemma?

Useful, if incomplete, guides and tools for making ethical decisions are the code of ethics for the EAP and other helping professions. All are available through the respective professional associations, including the EAPA. The ongoing and often difficult challenge faced by all counseling professionals is the application of ethical codes and principles. Discussing ethical quandaries with a colleague or supervisor while bearing in mind our obligations under our professional codes of ethics may be the most helpful and productive manner in which to resolve such issues. In this section, the discussion focuses on some of the common areas of ethical conflict encountered in EAP practice environments.

Privacy and Confidentiality

The professional obligations concerning the protection of client communications make up the most common area of ethics concerns faced by EA professionals. The expectation of confidentiality by consumers is based on the deeply held value of privacy. It is a right that is embodied in the U.S. Constitution. That intimate, highly personal communications will be kept private is a core component of meaningful counseling activity. The destruction of this expectation of privacy can disable both the specific counseling relationship and public trust in the counseling professions.

Confidentiality refers to the professional's obligation to maintain the privacy of therapeutic or consultative communications between a client and the professional. A key element of the code of ethics for all counseling professions, confidentiality is also embedded in the tenets of criminal law, and often in organizational policies.

Related to this broad concept is the more narrow one of privileged communication, a legal term that describes communications between professionals and clients that cannot be disclosed without the clients' specific permission. It is a right granted by statute to the consumer, not the professional. It is based on the principle that the public good is served if consumers are assured that trusted communications in the course of obtaining services from professionals will not be violated in legal proceedings. Long associated with patient-physician and client-attorney communications, the concept of privilege has recently been extended to some counseling relationships. Professionals must be aware of whether these statutes apply to them and, if so, that such privileges are not absolute.

So how are EA practitioners to operationalize confidentiality in their work with consumers and managers? Put simply, both consumers' identities as clients and the information professionals receive from them must be keep private. Such information must not be divulged to another party without the clients' permission, and professionals are obligated to ensure that their practice procedures and protocols comply with this obligation. They must also ensure that their employees, such as receptionists, appointment schedulers, transcriptionists, and billing services, also adhere to appropriate safeguards. Though confidentiality of client communications is both an ethical and legal obligation for the

EA practitioner, numerous exceptions require thoughtful and thorough consideration.

Duty to Report and Duty to Warn

Duty to report and duty to warn are two common categories of circumstances that call upon the EA professional to consider breaching the contract of client confidentiality. Both are based on the notion that the public good is better served by breaching the confidential nature of the client-professional communication in certain scenarios; that is, the service to the public outweighs the damage done to the individual. Legal and professional sanctions may be initiated against the EA professional who fails to report or warn.

Duty-to-report scenarios are often straightforward and relatively unambiguous. These reporting circumstances involve knowledge of physical or sexual abuse or neglect of a child. They are incorporated into statutes in all states and, in theory, apply to all citizens. A higher standard of reporting rigor is typically applied to members of the helping professions. In addition, some jurisdictions in recent years have expanded these statutes to apply to adult or elder abuse and neglect. This reporting duty is easily discharged through a telephonic communication to the jurisdiction-specific reporting agency or entity.

Prudent and ethical EA professionals are cognizant of applicable reporting statutes and procedures in their practice locations. Further, EA professionals should, as a part of their initial client education and orientation process, fully inform clients that statutes mandate the reporting of suspected abuse or neglect to appropriate authorities.

Duty-to-warn responsibilities were made evident to EA professionals through the famous Tarasoff ruling (*Tarasoff v. Regents of the University of California*, 1976). That ruling established the responsibility of counseling professionals to protect potential victims from violence by their clients. Although initially relevant only in California, other states have enacted a variety of Tarasoff-related statutes. All pertain to instances in which the counseling professional is made aware of the likelihood of imminent violence to an identifiable party. This duty may be discharged by, for example, warning the individual, such as a supervisor whose life has been threatened by the EA client; hospitalizing the client, through a civil or voluntary procedure; or altering the client's environment, such as taking measures to ensure that the client no longer has access to weapons or other means of violence.

EA professionals must address possible duty-to-warn circumstances thoroughly and thoughtfully. Professionals should be aware of the respective statutes in their areas of practice, and they should inform clients of such reporting obligations during the initial client orientation and education process. When facing a possible reporting scenario, the EA professional may consult with a colleague, a clinical supervisor or consultant, or legal counsel.

Subpoenas

A court subpoena is a legal document commanding the production of records, information, or testimony. Disregarding it or failing to respond in a timely manner can carry serious legal sanctions. This does not mean, however, that EA professionals must immediately disclose all client information.

Subpoenas are served or presented to the EA professional by a representative of the court issuing the document. Usually this is a law enforcement officer. The subpoena may command the production of copies of all records (both administrative and counseling) pertaining to the EA professional's interaction with a client, or only particular records, such as client contact notes, assessment forms, evaluative or screening tools, correspondence, or client self-assessment instruments. Subpoenas may also request that the professional appear in court to offer testimony about a client.

When presented with a subpoena, the prudent EA professional should follow the basic ethical axiom of considering what is in the best interest of the client. In this instance, it is best to inform the affected client that a court is legally commanding the production of sensitive, confidential information. Often clients are already aware that such actions may be initiated by attorneys in current court cases involving them. The professional should inform the client of the possible risks of disclosure of this information, and that the client may initiate a legal process to quash or invalidate the subpoena. The professional should advise the client that signing an authorization for such disclosures legally waives his or her privilege of confidentially in this instance.

If the EA client is disinclined to authorize disclosure, the EA professional should immediately consult legal counsel before responding to the court's subpoena. In that consultation with counsel, the EA professional should review the specific requests of the subpoena, the applicability of state statutes concerning privileged communication between the professional and client, the client's desires and expectations, and the possible consequences to the professional of noncompliance with the subpoena. Only after this consultation with counsel should the EA professional respond to the subpoena.

HOW TO DISCUSS CONFIDENTIALITY CONCERNS WITH EAP CLIENTS

Most clients are well aware that counseling received through their EAP, such as an assessment, follow-up interviews, or short-term counseling services, are provided by a structure that is sponsored and funded by their employer. This may naturally cause many clients to be concerned about the confidentiality of information they may reveal to a professional functioning under the auspices of an employer-sponsored EAP. This concern may arise when clients present voluntarily to use the EAP's face-to-face counseling services for themselves or their eligible family members. The concern may be heightened when their supervisor "suggests" that they see the EAP professional to obtain assistance with a problem that may be interfering with job performance. An even higher level of concern, one that may be destructive to a trustful therapeutic relationship, may exist in the case of mandatory referrals to the EAP.

This section provides suggested actions the EAP professional may employ to address these client concerns about confidentiality and help facilitate an effective utilization of EAP services.*

Educate the Client About the EAP

* The EAP is a resource provided by employers to assist employees and their families in resolving a wide range of problems.

---

*Material in this section is adapted from *Confidentiality and Employee Assistance Programs: What Every Employee Should Know.* Arlington, VA: EAPA, 1998, pp. 1-4.

- The EAP is staffed by professionals with special understanding of these unique programs and processes.
- EA professionals maintain ethical and legal obligations to their clients and patients, whether the referral and funding mechanism is an EAP or an employer-sponsored health care benefit program.
- EA professionals conduct themselves in accordance with a strict code of ethics. (Some EA professionals display the EAPA or other code of ethics; others may offer copies of the code to interested clients.)

Educate the Client About the Nature of Confidentiality in EAP Settings

- Protecting and preserving the confidentiality of client information, whether transmitted orally, in hard-copy form, or electronically, is a high priority for EA professionals. Without it, EAPs fail and professionals risk sanction.
- Information shared with an EA professional is confidential, but, as in other counseling contexts, this confidentiality is not absolute. (Not all employers understand the nature of confidentiality. It is the obligation of the EA professional to educate employer organizations as well to the extent and limitations of confidentiality of client information.)
- Similar to physicians, psychologists, and social workers, professionals functioning as EAP counselors are required by state and federal laws to report to appropriate authorities or individuals information shared by clients concerning imminent harm to themselves or others. Similar obligations exist concerning the threat of child or elder abuse and, in some states, spousal abuse.
- Due to public policy regarding the concern for the safety of American travelers, some federal agencies, and the industries regulated by them, have fitness-for-duty protocols that may require EA professionals to disclose information concerning unsafe activities that violate these regulations. The client working in such an industry should ask to review the employer's policy regarding the EAP and its confidentiality in these special circumstances.

Educate the Client About His or Her Rights As a Consumer

- If the client has been referred to the EAP by a supervisor, that person may want to know whether the client has kept the appointment or is participating in the EA professional's recommendation as to a plan of action to address a problem. This information may only be disclosed with the client's written permission.
- Other information may not be disclosed without another written permission statement from the client.
- The client has the right to understand what information is being released to any outside party.
- If the client has reason to believe that his or her confidentiality has been violated, the client may seek redress by contacting the EA professional's supervisor. Other avenues for redress include the EAP counselor's professional association, such as the EAPA; the professional's licensure governing body (often a branch of a state agency, board, or commission); or an attorney.

HEALTH CARE FRAUD:
HOW MANAGED CARE INVESTIGATES

The National Health Care Anti-Fraud Association (NHCAA) (2001) estimates dollars lost to health care fraud to be 3 to 10 percent of annual U.S. health care spending. In the extreme, this is approximately $100 billion lost to fraud out of a total of $1 trillion in U.S. health care spending (NHCAA, 2001). This figure far surpasses the total health care spending of most countries. Although it's estimated that only 2 percent of all health care providers engage in fraud, they do the most damage because they have the means, the opportunity, and the motive. Dishonest providers have the ability to commit fraud deliberately on a broad scale, spreading out their activities in their work with many patients and insurers. This makes detection more difficult. They have the ability to commit fraud frequently and regularly, resulting in large and illegal rewards at the expense of payers and consumers. Most dishonest health care professionals seem motivated simply by greed; others rationalize the exploitation of what they view as unfair payer systems.

Types of Fraud

Various types of fraud and abuse result in the illegal collection of funds by practitioners, facilities, or organizations, but two types are most common.

Billing for Services Not Rendered

The most common type of fraud committed by providers, this is estimated to account for 60 percent of all health care fraud cases. Billing for services not rendered may be as simple as billing for a therapy session that never took place. The author has witnessed some examples of this practice: a psychiatrist billing for services without seeing the patient, instead signing treatment progress notes written by others, and a practitioner who repeatedly billed for what was later determined to be more than twenty-four hours of therapy services in the workday.

Upcoding

Another common type of fraud, this is committed by deliberately billing for a more extensive service than was actually performed or provided to the patient. An example of upcoding is billing for a fifty-minute therapy session when only a twenty-minute session was performed. Another related type of fraud is *duplicate billing.*

Special Investigation Units (SIUs)

MCOs and MBHOs have as part of their mission the duty to ensure that funds intended for the payment of health care services are spent legitimately and appropriately and therefore, they establish processes to monitor this system. Most such organizations have SIUs that are responsible for detecting, preventing, and investigating suspected fraud and abuse. In addition, they work to recover funds lost to fraud and abuse, to protect clients' benefits, to meet state regulatory requirements, and to fulfill contractual obligations. They may work jointly on investigations with federal, state, and local law enforcement authorities and with customer health plan SIUs. One of their functions is to receive and investigate possible fraud or abuse reports.

Investigations into possible fraud or abuse by MCO or MBHO network providers are initiated in various ways. These reports are received from customers or consumers, care managers, customer service representatives, network managers, claims processing personnel, auditors, legal staff, EA and behavioral health care practitioners, and even the media. In addition, special fraud databases track, organize, and report investigations or sanctions.

SIUs coordinate their investigations closely with the MCOs' or MBHOs' legal departments, which ultimately determine whether legal action will be taken in any case. Cross-functional teams meet regularly to discuss open cases and progress in ongoing investigations. The outcome of these investigations can include practitioner or facility termination from network membership, licensure revocation proceedings, and criminal prosecution.

Estimated Financial Loss to Fraud

By its nature, the amount lost to health care fraud can never be quantified to the dollar. It can only be estimated, and such estimates vary widely.

In May, 1992, citing health insurance industry sources, the U.S. General Accounting Office (GAO) reported to Congress that the loss amounted to as much as an estimated 10 percent of the nation's total annual health care expenditure—or as much as $84 billion in 1992 alone. That "up to 10 percent" estimate remains common in 2000, at a time when annual U.S. health care spending totals more than $1 trillion. However, it does represent the high end of such estimates. Most NHCAA private insurers, for example, when asked their estimates of the proportion of health care dollars lost to outright fraud, placed that loss in a range of 3 to 5 percent (translation: annual loss of $30 billion to $50 billion of a $1 trillion expenditure). Furthermore, estimates of fraud losses often are mixed with broader estimates of "fraud, waste and abuse" in the health care system. In July 1997, based on the first comprehensive audit of Medicare claims paid, the Inspector General of the U.S. Department of Health and Human Services reported to Congress that approximately 14 percent of Medicare claims dollars—representing some $23 billion—were paid inappropriately, due to fraud and/or abuse and/or lack of medical documentation to support claims.

The bottom line: By whatever measure—even the lowest estimates—health care fraud is an enormous and intolerable drain on both our private and public health care systems.

Source: Estimated Financial Loss to Fraud Fact Sheet. National Health Care Anti-Fraud Association. Washington, DC. <www.nhcaa.org> Accessed March 25, 2002. Reprinted by permission of NHCAA.

Chapter 5

Marketing and Selling EAPs

Whether EA professionals practice in large MBHO settings where the EAP is only one of several products and is supported by a team of marketing and sales staff, or in small, EAP-focused practice environments where the practitioner is frequently both business owner and sole operator, all EA professionals are confronted with the formidable challenge of expanding their businesses. This may be achieved in two ways: (1) acquiring new customers, which increases the business's revenue stream, or (2) selling additional services to current or existing customers.

This sales challenge is particularly difficult for the EA practitioner who must both operate a business, addressing the demands of current clients and customers, and seek new customers. Many practitioners find themselves poorly equipped for this challenge. Most find that they must learn new sales skills and ways of approaching their enterprises due to a foundation of professional educational and practice experience that has too often focused entirely on the development of clinical, not sales, skills and competencies.

This chapter presents one straightforward means of approaching the development of an EAP sales strategy while building upon knowledge bases commonly possessed by EA and counseling professionals. Although it requires planning, research, and careful execution, it does not require any specialized sales expertise and is therefore applicable to a broad range of professionals and business settings. It will prepare the EAP company or EA practitioner for the implementation of direct sales efforts in an efficient, focused manner.

UNDERSTAND YOUR MARKET

A target market for EAP products is defined as potential customers who have a need (recognized or unrecognized) for EAP services *and* the resources to purchase these need-fulfilling services. The author's experience has been that most employers who are educated about the many benefits of EAP products appreciate the value of them, but that many simply do not have the resources to purchase the services. Therefore, these employers are not part of the market for EAP services.

Although services may of course be sold to purchasers outside the target market, defining and understanding your target market is imperative to focusing efforts and employing resources to their optimal advantage. Numerous ways exist to define and segment markets for EAP services, but two are illustrative.

First, practitioners may define a market by the size of the employer-purchaser. For example, services may be aimed at employers of fewer than 300 employees or those who employ more than 1,000 employees. Such divisions are based on the premise that the EAP needs of employers may differ by their size, and that employers of a certain size have commonalities of interest to those selling EAP products. A market populated by small employers may have fewer resources for benefit programs such as EAPs, and, therefore, the EA professional must address this reality by offering inexpensive services that deliver only core EAP technologies. Each market varies tremendously in a range of characteristics, so understanding the nature of the focus market is key.

Geography is another consideration when defining a market for EAP services. Do you intend to focus on local employers, or is your focus on serving employers in a region of a state, the entire state, or the nation? Defining a market geographically creates enormous diversity in that market. In this method of conceptualizing an EAP market, large employers are grouped with small businesses, unionized employers are grouped together with nonunion companies, and various, often unrelated industries are lumped together. Such a diverse collection of employer needs increases the challenge of finding need-satisfying EAP products because the only commonality is location.

However a market is defined, it must next be quantified so as to ensure that it is viable (i.e., having enough purchasing power to support an EAP business or community of EAP businesses). EA practitioners have available to them many sources for this type of information, including business directories, trade publications, chamber of commerce data, and a wealth of other sources of commercial information. Once the EA professional has defined and quantified the target market he or she is ready to create a focused plan for sales success.

DEVELOP CUSTOMER SUCCESS STORIES

Almost any new customer is curious about an EAP company's or EA practitioner's success with similar customers; this is the reason almost all new customers desire a list of references with whom they can verify the veracity of sales claims. Developing customer success stories, however, is much more than simply obtaining the permission of satisfied customers to use them as references. (This is, however, an important area, one often overlooked by practitioners. Professionals must maintain a list of current customers who are willing to serve as references and ensure that these clients are always notified prior to any call by a prospective new customer seeking information about the EAP supplier. Too many bids for new EAP business have gone awry when an embarrassed professional learns too late that a formerly satisfied customer no longer gives positive recommendations to a sales prospect!) Ensure that all references are, in effect, "success stories" who are more than happy to take time from their days to confer with a prospective purchaser of your EAP product and enthusiastically endorse your program and professionalism. If they promise anything less, eliminate them from your listing and find new references.

After developing the reference list and a methodology for its maintenance, EA professionals must address the generation and cataloging of success stories for the purpose of sales support. Success stories fall into two broad categories: employer success stories and end user success stories (i.e., EAP client stories, without attribution to any identifiable individual, that exemplify satisfaction with your EAP). These stories assist the sales process by giving prospective customers some assurance, through a narrative, that yours is a credible service and that has proved successful with a similar purchaser. Such success stories must then be woven into sales presentations; marketing materials, including abbreviated versions that may be integrated into brochures and flyers; and sales follow-up processes.

Employer Success Stories

Employer or purchaser success stories are brief written descriptions of an area of excellence noticed by a customer that are suitable for promotion. These stories should be well-written, concise, and truthful; carefully selected; and used with the customer's knowledge or, ideally, collaboration. Examples include topics such as flawless implementations, EAP response in a company crisis, or robust utilization of the EAP due to excellence in program promotion. Multiple employer success stories are needed to cover a range of topics of interest to new customers and to depict customers who are similar to the particular sales prospect.

How can EA professionals generate such success stories? Success stories of this type are best generated within the context of account management activities, that is, through a collaborative process of discussion with the customer concerning the aspects of the EAP that have been particularly innovative or satisfying. Other source material, for such stories are customer-generated letters of appreciation or commendation for work well-done or acknowledgments of particularly strong contributions by an EA professional.

End User Success Stories

End user success stories are of a more personal and sometimes emotional nature. They often connect strongly with lay purchasers who cannot fully appreciate the technical rigors of a quality EAP but can identify with an instance in which a counseling professional has impacted an individual's life in a meaningful way. These stories, which can contain no client-identifying information, must meet the previously stated criteria for veracity, clarity, and relevance to the purchaser, while typifying how the EAP impacts individual consumers. Counseling success stories, summaries of crisis interventions, or satisfied wellness program participants are common examples.

How can EA professionals generate these types of program success stories? The most straightforward way to generate such stories is through an integration of sales and client satisfaction or quality assurance efforts. EA professionals must employ a coherent client or end user satisfaction evaluation system. Such efforts may range from modest mail-in surveys completed by EAP service users to elaborate, costly, but scientifically valid telephonic surveys of thousands of consumers. Regardless of the method, any such client satisfaction process, if properly structured, can yield numerous examples of how the EAP made a difference to end users or their families.

Another method for the collection of such stories is to obtain feedback from supervisors or managers who have had success in using the program to assist a troubled worker or to teach new skills through an EAP educational service. Supervisors and managers are a key stakeholder group within any organization and are often viewed by purchasers as a powerful voice in evaluating a prospective new service. Their endorsement of an EAP product, professional, or company based on an actual workplace scenario may be particularly influential in some sales processes.

Tracking and Communicating Success Stories

In the course of a consultation with an EA professional, the author once asked the owner about the organization's customer success stories. The owner of the EAP firm replied that the organization had numerous such success stories, but they just didn't document them! This is a common problem in not only EAP practices but in many human service fields. Professionals often receive words or letters of appreciation from consumers and customers or collect evaluations from participants in educational seminars or psychoeducational classes and then fail to integrate this valuable material into their sales processes. Management personnel in larger organizations often fail to communicate the need for such information to the direct service personnel and thus fail to take advantage of opportunities to collect meaningful client service stories.

EA professionals, then, must analyze how best to collect success stories in their setting, develop a method for tracking these stories, and decide how to communicate these successes throughout the organization, however large or small. This two-way communication of success stories throughout an organization has the benefits of both improving morale and building teamwork while striving toward new sales and growth.

An easily implemented example of how this may be achieved is the "case of the month" process. In this process, staff or colleagues are asked and given incentives to submit a brief description of a particularly positive case outcome. In an EAP setting, this may pertain to a counseling or crisis intervention scenario, a consultation with a supervisor, a training event, or a CISD episode. Cases selected as outstanding may then be shared throughout the organization and may be edited and refined as part of the catalog of customer success stories.

DETERMINE THE KEY DECISION MAKERS IN AN EAP PURCHASE

To achieve EAP sales success, professionals must understand who in their target markets are the decision makers concerning an EAP purchase, and how the EAP organization can best communicate with them. Proactive EAP companies carry on some level of communication about their services with prospective customers' key decision makers. At the same time, few professionals or companies have the time or resources to waste in misdirected communication efforts, so careful consideration of this point is in order.

Decision makers may be divided into two groups: decision influencers and actual decision makers. Decision influencers are frequently, though not exclusively, agents external to the purchaser. For example, a benefits consultant or broker may not actually make the purchase decision for the customer company but may exert a strong influence as to the EAP vendor finally selected. The benefits consultant may select finalists from a larger group of EAP suppliers to bring to the prospective customer as candidates in the EAP sales process. The consultant may also serve as a technical resource to the customer and may assist the customer in proposal evaluation, vendor interviews, and vendor office or site visits. Another example of decision influencers common to EAPs pertains to managed behavioral health care sales processes in which the purchaser's EAP supplier assists the purchaser in the evaluation of behavioral health care services. Other decision influencers include internal stakeholders, such as supervisors, managers, labor leadership, and occupational medicine personnel, as well as other customers, other vendors, insurance, health care or health plan sales staff, and professional colleagues and associates.

Decision makers are the actual purchaser representatives charged with the responsibilities of selecting (or recommending selection to the company's top management) the EAP supplier and of negotiating and finalizing the supplier's contract. In larger work organizations, this is often a cross-functional team, sometimes guided by the organization's purchasing department, which oversees the entire process to ensure adherence to company policies concerning a fair selection process. Other members of such teams often include representatives from various relevant functional areas within the company, such as human resources, benefits, finance, safety, training, and occupational medicine departments. Naturally, in smaller organizations, this important decision-making responsibility may fall on one individual, such as a human resources manager, benefits manager, or even the president of the organization.

To improve the prospects of sales success, EA professionals must understand their target markets' decision influencers and decision makers and then make plans to communicate with them according to their nature. This can best be accomplished by developing a communication plan after determining the answers to the following questions:

- Who are the key decision makers for EAP purchases in our target market?
- Who are the key influencers of EAP purchase decisions in our target market?
- How many of these individuals are in our target market?
- Do we have a mailing list of these individuals?
- Can mailing lists be generated or purchased and at what expense?
- What process do we have to identify and update our list of these individuals?
- How do we communicate with these individuals?
- What methods of influencing these individuals have been successful in our past—direct mail, telemarketing, personal visits, electronic media?
- What are the best strategies and tactics to influence these individuals?
- How important is it for us to influence these individuals?

Determine What Advertising Decision Makers Read

Most organizations have few advertising dollars to waste on misguided attempts to influence decision makers, so EA professionals are wise to analyze carefully what types of advertising, if any, gain exposure with EAP purchasers. Even with a limited budget, advertising can create awareness and influence decision makers if it is properly targeted. To target advertising properly, the EA professional must consider several questions:

- What are the financial and budgetary constraints for any advertising program?
- What advertising might EAP purchasing decision makers in our target market read?
- Has the EAP organization advertised in the past and with what measurable results?
- Have we partnered with other companies or organizations in the past in our advertising efforts?
- What sorts of free advertising—new releases, print media interviews, television or radio interviews, gratis service offerings, or public speaking engagements—have been utilized and how might they be integrated into an advertising program?
- What is the role of an Internet Web site in advertising directed toward our target market?

Determine What Trade Shows, Conferences, or Professional Meetings Decision Makers Attend

Various professional meetings are an important venue for advertising services and meeting prospective customers. By identifying these opportunities, EA professionals may selectively advertise services through conference schedules or literature, provide display literature and product information at vendor booths, or simply meet prospective customers and build relationships. Costs for implementing such a strategy vary greatly. Some organizations prohibit vendors from attendance or participation unless they qualify for membership in the sponsoring organization. Sometimes prospective decision makers or influencers choose to attend the same continuing professional education events as EA professionals, so sellers must be aware to review attendee lists, when available, and use the events to meet prospective customers. In adding a professional meeting facet to an overall sales strategy, EA professionals should analyze answers to the following questions:

- Do EAP purchasers, decision makers, or decision influencers in our target market attend any trade shows, professional meetings, or conferences?
- Can our EAP organization make a list of such events?
- What motivates such attendance—required professional education, industry awareness, social and professional interests?
- Can our EAP organization conduct an analysis of the cost of advertising and/or attending these events?
- Are there restrictions as to who may attend or participate in these events?
- How can we influence purchasers through a professional meeting facet of our sales strategy, and what are the costs and benefits of such an initiative?

Chapter 6

Innovations in Managed Care

MBHO systems are dynamic entities that respond to market and customer needs. This chapter describes three of numerous innovative programs aimed at the customers who purchase managed care services for their employees or enrollees. Two are aimed directly at building on existing MBHO services. The third is offered by a company in the related field of providing informational and educational services to employees or health plan members, in this instance, via the Internet.

MBHO PSYCHOPHARMACOLOGY MANAGEMENT SERVICES

The managed care industry continues to innovate programs and services to meet the changing needs of purchasers, such as insurance carriers and employers, who self-fund insurance products for employees and their dependents. One such service is a behavioral health pharmacy management program, which assists customers in more effectively managing psychotropic drug utilization and the escalating costs of medications used to treat psychiatric disorders.

Behavioral health pharmacy management programs attempt to achieve two ambitious goals:

1. Assist PCPs and psychiatrists in providing the best practices in behavioral health medication management
2. Help customers (insurance companies, employers, or labor organizations) reduce total health care costs through reducing the costs of psychotropic medications while improving patients' quality of life

To address these goals, these programs employ one or more strategies, including education or targeted interventions aimed at improving behavioral health prescribing practices on the part of PCPs or psychiatrists; paid-claims data analysis aimed at identifying problems and trends in the prescription patterns of psychotropic medications; and active clinical intervention aimed at increasing or improving the clinical outcomes for individual patients through improved behavioral health prescribing.

Education

Education aimed at *practitioners* is focused on influencing and improving behavioral health prescribing patterns. The educational efforts of MCOs to manage psychopharmacy involve techniques designed to reduce increasing drug costs associated with inappropriate diagnosis of behavioral health disorders and/or improper prescribing of prescription drugs for the treatment of behavioral health disorders. This is a daunting and challenging task, one that, to some extent, must offset and overcome the substantial efforts of the pharmacy industry—which each year expends large resources through a variety of avenues—aimed at influencing physician prescribing patterns. Some methods used by the pharmacy industry include the following:

- Physician office visits by pharmaceutical company sales representatives
- Sponsorship and other financial support or inducements for continuing education events, conferences, and professional association gatherings
- Promotional giveaways to physicians and office staff, such as pens, calendars, and other items
- Medication samples
- Advertisements in the professional and trade literature
- Direct advertising of prescription medications to the general public, who in turn may request of their physicians prescriptions for specific name-brand medications

Based on years of experience with PCPs prescribing substantial amounts of antidepressants nationwide, MCOs have developed dosing guidelines for specific types of common psychotropic medications, such as antidepressants. These guidelines educate and assist physicians and are targeted at specific prescribing problems commonly seen in the primary care office setting. Guidelines and intervention materials can be made available for various important clinical variables, such as starting a dose too low or too high, inappropriate dosage titration, and premature discontinuation of pharmacotherapy. This education-based intervention can empower PCPs and improve the quality and appropriateness of medication usage, while reducing costs to purchasers. Such a program may be employed with a panel of physicians or on a more limited, targeted basis. For example, paid-claims information may be analyzed to identify unusual or outlier prescribing patterns and a letter communicating this information may be generated to the particular physician. Included in the intervention letter are the drug dosing guidelines and supportive information. Continued monitoring and follow-up as needed assists such outlier prescribers to moderate their patterns.

Educating *consumers* about behavioral health medications is another aspect of behavioral health pharmacy management programs, and it is made more complex by the nature of the illness being treated, as all who have treated psychiatric patients well know. Unlike many of the more purely medical illnesses, behavioral health conditions often require chronic or even lifelong medication regimen. Medication noncompliance by patients has been a difficult issue for health care practitioners to address effectively. Stigma, costs, poor attendance at needed treatment sessions, poor coordination between treatment facilities and practitioners, and apparent or perceived deleterious side effects associated with medications serve as powerful deterrents to compliance with the desired treatment regime. In many instances, patients with serious behavioral health diagnoses have their psychotropic medication prescriptions filled at a pharmacy but never take them. This hinders the efforts to improve patients' conditions, creates an enormous amount of waste in the health care system, and is very costly to insurers and employers.

One facet, then, of any effective educational program involves activities to improve patient compliance, or a so-called drug compliance aspect of the overall program. This component may include a multiyear program of consumer-friendly educational materials, in multiple formats, such as written, electronic, and audiovisual forms, to be sent to consumers at critical junctures, once anyone is identified as being placed on a particular psychotropic medication. Obtaining the active support of significant family members in such efforts is also key. Consumers may be referred to this program by the prescribing physician or they may self-enroll. To be successful, this aspect of the program should demonstrate maximized medication compliance, provide evidence-enhanced patient education, and document influencing the behavior of health care practitioners in preventing patients from relapse or treatment failure due to medication noncompliance. In addition, such programs must also serve as a time-saving tool for busy health care practitioners while achieving an optimized treatment outcome for their patients and their families. Creative linkages with insurers' disease management programs, school health services, EAP, and employers' occupational health departments enhance the prospects of compliance and success, and offering the educational program in other nonmedical settings can also support patients' overall functioning.

Paid-Claims Data Analysis

Psychopharmacy management programs partner with purchasers and their pharmacy benefit managers (PBMs) in performing an in-depth analysis of aggregate psychopharmacy claims. (A PBM is another specialty service supplier who oversees the administration of the purchaser's entire pharmacy benefit.) Utilization of behavioral health drugs can be analyzed for trends, norms, and outliers. These data can then be integrated into an executive summary report that identifies customer-specific behavioral health pharmacy solutions. For example, reports can be generated to capture:

- fraud and abuse by health care professionals,
- inappropriate prescribing,
- multiple prescribers,
- polypharmacy,
- poor compliance, and
- therapeutic duplication.

In an effort to improve efficacy, MBHOs can also work with customers and their PBMs to review prospective and concurrent drug utilization review (DUR) programs and processes currently in place for behavioral health care medicines. Retrospective DUR processes monitor physician prescribing patterns to ensure appropriate use of medications through a concerted focus upon the following:

- *Appropriate therapy*—Does the diagnosis justify the prescribed treatment?
- *Dosing parameters*—Was the patient placed on a psychotropic medication at an appropriate starting dose, and has the dose been titrated upward to achieve the optimal therapeutic outcome?
- *Duration of therapy*—Did the patient receive an adequate trial of medication before increasing the dose or changing medications? For example, for the treatment of major depressive disorder, was the patient treated appropriately during the acute and continuation phases of treatment?
- *Duplication of therapy*—Is the patient receiving more than one drug for the same condition, and, if so, is it medically justified (i.e., polypharmacy versus augmentation therapy)?

The purpose of this analysis is to identify prescribing outliers and monitor behavioral health-related drug utilization. Based on these findings, MBHOs can make recommendations to customers concerning a joint effort to manage effectively the use of psychotropic medications.

Active Clinical Intervention

MBHOs can also assist customers in developing clinical intervention programs. This aspect of the program can focus on issues such as polypharmacy, inappropriate dosing, and drug compliance, first through a retrospective DUR process. The second step in such a clinical intervention program is the development of evidenced-based, clear treatment guidelines for behavioral health-related disorders, such as depression, schizophrenia, and attention deficit hyperactivity disorder (ADHD). The order of development and implementation can be based on the needs of any particular customer.

An MCO may apply its clinical expertise in behavioral health drug therapy to assist in formulary management. MCO staff may participate in customers' pharmacy and therapeutics committees, which review treatment guidelines, protocols, and clinical management associated with psychotropic drugs used in health plan settings. The MCO psychiatrist on this committee can provide clinical reviews of the existing psychotropic formulary medications as well as of newer agents as they enter the market. Furthermore, MCO staff can assist health plans in developing clinical protocols to ensure the appropriate usage of these newer and more expensive agents by PCPs.

PBM Collaboration

Finally, MBHOs may collaborate with customers' PBMs to provide oversight of PBM activities associated with psychotherapeutic agents. This type of oversight includes quality checks on DUR edits, prior authorization criteria, days supply of medication, therapeutic duplication, multiple prescribers, and multiple pharmacies.

Impacting behavioral health care pharmacy costs is a complex and resource-laden endeavor. It pertains to a broad array of actions that may be integrated in multiple systems to maximize their impact. If pharmacy costs continue to escalate, interventions to manage them will likely become more prevalent, creative, and varied.

INNOVATIONS: USES OF THE INTERNET IN MBHO ENVIRONMENTS

Magellan Behavioral Health

The Internet has opened up unlimited—many yet unforeseen—possibilities, particularly in the area of EAPs and managed behavioral health care. Magellan Behavioral Health, the Columbia, Maryland-based industry giant, is using the Internet to expand its service availability and utility to both the member-consumer and the practitioner communities.

Regarding the member-consumer, this MBHO company recognized that, although many advances have occurred in the past few years, the stigma surrounding behavioral health continues to be a core issue, as many in need of services do not access care or information about care as a direct result (U.S. DHHS, 1999). Recognizing this and other issues of access, Magellan, working with a strategic partner, created in 2000 an enhanced, highly interactive Internet utility designed to focus on skill building and problem resolution. The dynamic potential offered through this medium is comprehensive. The interactive capability is readily available, twenty-four hours a day, seven days a week, and includes interactive content, online practitioner directories, specific coverage information, and available resources, including those in the community and online links.

Magellan's Internet technology allows participants accurate, current information, point-to-point referral procedures, and self-guided programs to help people help themselves. Their goal is to reach individuals through confidential assistance at home or in the workplace to help them address problems and build skills before they require higher-level or more intensive, more expensive services. Their system's interactivity empowers users and delivers essential tools directed toward achieving healthier lifestyles. This interactivity is accomplished through numerous self-improvement programs covering issues of daily living, such as stress, depression, and anxiety; personal growth topics, such as time management, coping with change, and life planning; and health and wellness issues, such as diet, nutrition, and exercise.

Magellan's system is designed to provide something relevant to everyone. They focus on preventive, early intervention to reach people at the initial stages of the care continuum, who are not presently in treatment, and also as an adjunct to psychotherapy for those who are. Consensus in the behavioral health care industry is that when individuals are reached early, they are more likely to make changes in their lives. The smart technology used to create such interactive programs builds upon the direct information supplied by the users and is designed to engage them in dialogue, allowing them to create a tailored plan to self-improvement. As such, the programs utilize conditional logic, branching to demonstrate a personalized, truly interactive site, unlike others in behavioral health and well beyond purely informational sites with simple assessment tools.

Members can access these services through the following processes:

- Quick information programs provide straightforward, well-organized information on a wide range of health and personal development areas. Features include help getting started, quick facts, helpful hints, answers to frequently asked questions, and resources for further assistance, including referral to EAP and behavioral health care assessment and counseling services.

- Health plan-related information is customized for Magellan's customers and includes a description of benefits, how to access the program, frequently asked questions, and practitioner directories.

- Self-assessments are single-session, fifteen- to twenty-minute programs that ask questions, summarize responses, and provide recommendations for addressing specific problem areas. These are designed to give the user an objective appraisal of his or her problem and its severity, as well as an opportunity for self-exploration and links to available information.

- Personal plan programs are single-session, twenty- to thirty-minute programs designed to teach users about a topic or problem area and to provide tools with which the user can improve his or her situation. A typical program includes information, skill training, demonstrations, online exercises, and homework.

- Coached series programs take interactive online services one step further, offering multisession programs with individual coaching assembled and monitored by a licensed mental health professional. These models use six to ten online sessions that begin with an online questionnaire, utilizing the principles of cognitive behavior therapy, and then offer coaching and feedback from a mental health counselor throughout the course of the sessions.

In addition to the available programs, an additional range of self-help options includes community resources links and information, live chat and discussion groups, message boards, and *Click! Online Magazine.* Each of these services provide vehicles to ask and respond to questions on health and skill-building issues. The discussion rooms also feature a monthly guest speaker who is a leading expert in the particular topic area being discussed.

The system architecture has been built and integrated using the latest Web technologies, with each functional system structured using a three-tier design examined and approved by Microsoft. The front tier runs on Microsoft Internet Information Server (IIS 4.0) and contains Active Server Pages (ASP), VBScript, JavaScript and HTML that is compliant with all browsers currently in use. The middle tier, which is key to achieving necessary scalability, was built using a Microsoft Transaction Server (MTS) and communicates with the database. The back tier, or database, contains hundreds of tables running on Microsoft Sequel Server.

Magellan, through Epotec its partner company, works with EMC2, a leading national Web hosting service and data management company, and VeriSign, the world leader in encryption technology which provides the security functions. They utilize forty-bit data encryption whenever personal data are transferred via the Internet, using a secure server certificate from VeriSign. Further, the database is not directly connected to the Internet; rather, it resides on a machine completely separate from the Web and transaction servers. Access to the database and transfer of data to and from it takes place via a virtual private network (VPN), using 128-bit data encryption.

Enhancements

The Magellan Behavioral Health product will soon offer a client-specific messaging system that will allow Magellan's care managers to communicate directly with participants enrolled in the system. After a member sends a message through the system, it will enter a queue, and the next available Magellan care manager will handle it. This provides a confidentiality aspect not available through an e-mail system and can be utilized anywhere in the world.

Magellan's vision for online connectivity with practitioners includes the development of an enhanced platform utilizing practice management tools for practitioners to access eligibility data, claims status, treatment planning, and scheduling tools online in real time. The site also provides claims submission capabilities and houses Magellan's regularly evaluated and updated medical necessity criteria, clinical practice guidelines, practitioner handbook, practitioner focus newsletter, and other information concerning Magellan-related news and events.

As this project continues, they intend to launch private communication centers (chat rooms) for peers and industry experts and an extensive searchable database of professional resources, associations, journal articles, and more. Through this effort, they further intend to offer continuing education programs via online courses for all disciplines.

In addition, practitioners can utilize the consumer content portion of this site to serve as an adjunct to traditional therapy. Participants can access this site to make use of the personal plans and/or self-assessment programs as homework between therapy sessions. This feature offers hands-on activities, informing and empowering individuals to assist themselves in advancing through treatment.

A demonstration of this Web site can be found at <www.magellan care.com>.

MyDailyHealth

Responding to dramatically rising health care costs, coupled with a demand for technology-based solutions, MyDailyHealth, now affiliated with ProAct Technologies, takes wellness to the electronic super-highway. Through the Chapel Hill, North Carolina-based company's site, users can access—and even receive—health information customized to their individual circumstances.

MyDailyHealth is an online, one-stop source for consolidated corporate health promotion and other applications for use by employees and their families. MyDailyHealth's platform of services provides corporate employees a unique, rewards-driven, programmatic preventive health experience that encourages behavior and lifestyle modifications through its interactive applications and context-sensitive features.

In developing its advanced technology engines and interactive incentives system, ProAct has created a unique user experience that promises high rates of member retention while allowing employers to track risks and behaviors. On a daily basis, employees are encouraged to visit their personalized Web pages to retrieve fresh, relevant content in accordance with their individual preferences. The MyDailyHealth experience allows each employee to earn "Healthy Points," redeemable for valuable, health-oriented awards and incentives. Using health promotion as a lead, ProAct intends to enhance its application offerings to provide a total interactive corporate health management delivery platform.

Presently, the MyDailyHealth application platform focuses on health promotion, fitness, nutrition, lifestyle management, and recovery. Current development initiatives include more robust pharmaceutical, disease, and condition management work tools. Future development will explore such areas as interactive training and career advancement tools.

ProAct's primary market includes Fortune 1000 corporations and other large organizations, managed care companies, and health promotion providers. MyDailyHealth applications are licensed to the customer organization on a per employee or per member per year (PMPY) basis. Individual employees receive the program as a benefit from their employer/insurer at no additional charge. To date, the company has signed licensing agreements with several organizations, including Allina Health System Foundation and Intracorp.

Critical to the success of MyDailyHealth and its customers' corporate health promotion programs is the ability to deliver above-average membership retention. ProAct found early success in creating a user experience that promotes repeat usage at a higher rate than presently experienced by other consumer e-health services. The following key components of the site encourage membership retention:

- *Interactivity*—Creating a rich, programmatic, daily interactive experience is core to building user loyalty. ProAct developed its proprietary database engine to create and serve customized pages based on user-selected categories of interest. The site interface includes My Check-In and My ScoreCard features that provide guidance and real-time feedback on pages visited and incentive points accumulated.
- *Content*—MyDailyHealth contains fresh, relevant content derived from best-of-breed third-party sources supplemented with high-quality original material. The content covers health, fitness, recovery, and behavior and disease management, presented in a daily ten- to fifteen-minute experience. MyDailyHealth also uses programmatic wellness tools designed to promote daily behavior management. As the site evolves, ProAct will develop additional applications.
- *Awards*—Users redeem accumulated Healthy Points for health- and wellness-related awards. Employers can tailor the customizable Healthy Points system around areas where they would like to drive more traffic. To ensure the success of the incentive pro-

gram, the company handles all distribution and promotion of the awards.

These elements have met with success in both attracting users within companies and increasing retention. Through the first quarter of 2000, over 18 percent of MyDailyHealth's users returned for repeated visits. It is expected that, as the full version of the incentive engine is rolled out to all sites, the percentage will increase dramatically.

Features

MyDailyHealth's "Ten Minutes a Day to a Healthy, Active Life" program is built around three hubs: wellness, fitness, and nutrition. The key components are found conveniently in the My Check-In navigation section. Here, users are encouraged to set health goals, create a personal wellness program, and earn points for participating in the site's features on a daily basis. Some of the main components are as follows:

- *My Wellness Center*—includes general health and wellness news, daily health tips, quotes, and question and answer features
- *My Nutrition Watch*—provides nutritional tips, news, and "The Healthy Cook," a dynamic, fully searchable recipe and menu finder
- *My Fitness Coach*—encourages physical health through daily exercise and fitness; includes various fitness tips, news, and "Daily Deskercises"—personalized, illustrated daily aerobics for the user's home or office
- *Daily Doses*—daily motivational selections for weight management, stress reduction, smoking cessation, and general health and fitness
- *Pharma Check-In*—customizeable tool to assist users in taking medication
- *News and Discussion*—discussion groups, member e-mail, and question and answer forums

Recovery and Lifestyle Management—MyDailyRecovery.com

MyDailyHealth's first application, MyDailyRecovery.com, provides information and work tools for individuals recovering from chemical and emotional dependencies. The site uses an interactive online format to promote healing and personal growth on a daily basis. Initially conceived as a subscription-based service, MyDaily Recovery.com is specifically focused on lifestyle management, behavior modification, and supplemental aftercare. Developed over the course of 1997, MyDailyRecovery.com was launched in April 1998.

Critical to treating destructive dependencies is replacing negative behaviors with constructive, enriching relationships. MyDailyRecovery offers individuals a secure, confidential place to gain information, access resources, and work on their personal goals. Feature include a personalized Daily Check-In, discussion groups, news, anonymous e-mail, Daily Doses, self-help and self-assessment tools, book reviews, and an array of community resources designed specifically to take advantage of the uniquely interactive qualities of the Internet. Because of the importance of recovery, MyDailyRecovery is also offered to the general public for a minimal monthly fee.

Appendix A

2001 Directory of Major North American MBHO and EAP Companies

Company	Headquarters Location	Contact Information
Magellan Behavioral Health	Columbia, MD	800.788.4005 www.magellanhealth.com
ValueOptions	Falls Church, VA	800.397.1630 www.valueoptions.com
Managed Health Network	San Rafael, CA	800.541.3353 www.mhn.com
CIGNA Behavioral Health (formerly MCC Behavioral Care)	Eden Prairie, MN	800.926.2273 www.cignabehavioral.com
Ceridian Performance Partners	Minneapolis, MN	800.788.1949 www.ceridianperformance.com
APS Healthcare	Bethesda, MD	800.752.7242 www.apscare.com
ComPsych Corporation	Chicago, IL	800.515.6159 www.compsych.com
Integra	King of Prussia, PA	800.232.1540 www.integra-ease.com
FEI Behavioral Health (formerly Family Enterprises)	Milwaukee, WI	414.359.1055 www.feinet.com
VMC Behavioral Healthcare Services	Gurnee, IL	800.843.1327 www.vmceap.com

Source: Adapted from Practice Strategies. Cary, NC. 6(8). 2000 Page 5.

Appendix B

Sample EAP Sales Proposal
for a New Customer

In this sample proposal response, our fictional EAP is called the 21st Century EAP Company. Once documented, 21st Century edits and tailors this template to serve as a foundation for specific responses from various potential customers of EAP services.

THE 21ST CENTURY EAP COMPANY

The 21st Century EAP Company is a recognized leader in the development and administration of cost-effective and efficient EAPs. At 21st Century, we understand that the value to employers of an EAP as an early intervention strategy lies in its ability to provide crisis intervention, early problem identification and resolution before the problem reaches crisis level, and support of your organization in dealing with performance issues. These actions will translate into a more productive workforce.

The 21st Century EAP Company always employs a proactive approach to employee assistance and care. We know that some employees need assistance that we can readily identify, and we then locate resources for them in the community. We also know that sometimes employees may need care that requires more extensive clinical expertise. The 21st Century EAP Company matches your employees' needs through our clinical expertise and network of services and practitioners. The 21st Century EAP Company will provide effective, qualitative services through assessment and referral into short-term counseling or, when indicated, into the customer's mental health and substance abuse benefit plan.

Participants need timely and immediate access to high-quality and cost-effective care. They need access to services that are responsive to their needs. It is important that customer employees understand and feel comfortable with using all the services available through their Employee Assistance Program. The 21st Century EAP Company is committed to educating employees about the benefits of receiving EAP direction and assistance. We are prepared to provide orientations to familiarize your management and other key individuals with our EAP services, as well as key contact individuals who will serve customer employees.

Our EAP service offers the following characteristics:

- Access to a twenty-four-hour, seven-day, toll-free EAP help and referral line staffed by 21st Century EAP Company's EAP specialists
- Initial assessment by the 21st Century EAP Company EAP specialist and referral to an appropriate practitioner within the customer's mental health practitioner network
- Referral to community services for needs not met through counseling by the mental health network practitioner
- Promotion of EAP services to the customer through orientation sessions and educational materials
- Training of the customer's managers and supervisors on the use of the EAP
- Orientation of the customer's senior management through briefing sessions
- Confidentiality of services
- Management reporting
- Satisfaction surveys for the customer

Our EAP products have proven cost-effective for diverse public- and private-sector customers, as well as major national and regional employers. When you purchase 21st Century EAP Company's Employee Assistance Program services, you are investing in the quality of your work environment. By offering alternatives for assessment, problem solving, and referral, you are helping customer employees resolve personal problems before they become job performance problems.

PRODUCT OFFERINGS

Our major managed behavioral care products include the following:

- *Employee Assistance Programs:* A confidential assessment, counseling, and referral program designed to address personal and workplace problems is offered to customer employees and their families at no cost. The EAP also includes a supervisory assistance component.
- *Managed Behavioral Health:* This program is designed to manage Mental Health/Substance Abuse (MH/SA) treatment across the entire

continuum of care. 21st Century EAP Company offers utilization review programs as well as network-based programs.

21st Century EAP Company has the necessary financial stability and product and staff credibility necessary to ensure contract performance for your employees.

COMMITMENT TO ACCREDITATION

21st Century EAP Company has made a commitment to accreditation through the Employee Assistance Society of North America's (EASNA) EAP Accreditation Program. Accreditation through this prestigious EAP-specific and rigorous program assures our customers of our EAP expertise and depth of quality. In fact, senior 21st Century EAP staff members are EASNA Site Reviewers for this accreditation program and process.

21st Century EAP Company has also demonstrated a strong commitment to the National Committee on Quality Assurance (NCQA) accreditation and to the advancement of quality standards for organizations engaged in the behavioral health care service delivery industry. Accreditation of our behavioral care services enhances the quality and depth of EAP services that we will provide to your employees and managers.

OVERVIEW OF THE EAP PRODUCT

21st Century EAP Company's EAP model offers employers the attractive benefits of assessment and situational counseling, including crisis intervention; unlimited management consultations; wellness workshops; drug-free workplace programs; and, when needed, critical incident stress debriefings. Customer, dependents, and supervisors can access our services by calling a toll-free number that is staffed around the clock by licensed clinicians with on-call access to psychiatrist supervisors and consultants. This ease of access encourages early problem identification and intervention.

Initial telephone assessments are conducted by our staff EAP specialists, who work with customer employees and their dependents to identify and access the most appropriate resources for problem resolution. Following assessment, employees and/or dependents are referred to appropriate community resources, to our EAP network practitioners for situational counseling, or (for more serious psychiatric or substance abuse problems) to their MH/SA benefits for longer-term therapy.

Toll-Free Help Line

21st Century EAP Company operates a nationwide, twenty-four-hour, toll-free help line for customer employees and dependents who need information and routine or emergency services. Our help line extends its services to all persons, including supervisors or employees' family members, who may need to refer an employee for assistance; it also is available to practitioners seeking authorizations for coverage of EAP services. The simplicity of calling one number to gain access to the full continuum of EAP and MH/SA services encourages early referral among your employees and their dependents.

Twenty-Four-Hour, 365-Day Availability

21st Century EAP Company's toll-free help line is available twenty-four hours a day, 365 days a year for customer employees and their families to access EAP referral services. This telephone line is available and accessible nationwide.

21st Century EAP Company's Client Service Representatives (CSRs) serve as the initial points of contact for all our behavioral health and EAP service callers. For routine calls, these specialists initiate the intake process by gathering basic demographic information, confirming eligibility when needed or requested by customer (we assume eligibility for any EAP caller accessing services via your dedicated toll-free number), and answering benefits- or product-related questions. All demographic and clinical information is entered immediately into our online clinical information system.

Callers requesting short-term counseling services are transferred to EAP specialists, who conduct the initial intake interview prior to referral for an EAP assessment. All EAP specialists are licensed, experienced clinicians; they remain on-site around the clock.

Short-Term Counseling

Counseling is available through one of two basic models: the *assessment and referral* model which offers up to three counseling sessions, and the *short-term treatment* model, which most commonly offers five to eight sessions. In determining which model to recommend to a prospective customer, we begin by obtaining information about clinical and financial objectives relative to the EAP. If short-term treatment is desired, we usually recommend a five-session *per employee/dependent per year* model. We favor this configuration because EAP professionals are aware that most situational problems can be resolved within a brief number of sessions. If problems can be resolved within the EAP, fewer referrals ultimately need to be made to costlier MH/SA benefits, reducing costs to our customer while addressing employees' concerns through a single, simple program.

Initial Assessment and Referral

When a caller (employee or dependent or household member) requests clinical services, our CSR routes the call and the online eligibility information directly to an EAP specialist, who assumes responsibility for assessment, referral, service authorization, and ongoing care monitoring. The EAP specialist determines the urgency of the caller's needs according to the following definitions:

- *Critical Emergency:* A life-threatening situation in which the caller is threatening imminent harm to self or another person, such as a family member, supervisor, or co-worker. The EAP caller in this circumstance states or implies that he or she is not in control of these impulses. The telephone services described previously are followed, and emergency help is dispatched immediately to the EAP caller's location, or care is arranged in an emergency room or other acute crisis setting.
- *Emergency:* A nonlife-threatening situation involving a caller who states or implies that he or she may do harm to self or another person if help is not received immediately. The caller states or implies the need for help but is able to maintain impulse control for several hours until help can be arranged. Face-to-face emergency services of some type should be provided to the EAP client within six hours.
- *Urgent:* A situation in which the EAP caller is experiencing a loss of control and is feeling increasingly frustrated over various life events. The resultant plan involves problem avoidance activity, such as running away or using or abusing substances, rather than threatening harm to self, family members, friends, supervisors, or co-workers. An urgent situation requires that face-to-face counseling services be offered and provided within forty-eight hours.
- *Routine:* A situation in which the caller's condition is sufficiently stable to allow a longer period between referral and the first face-to-face contact without negative impact on the caller's condition or motivation to enter treatment. The appointment time offered is within five to ten business days of the request for service.

During the initial telephone contact, the 21st Century EAP Company EAP specialist conducts an initial assessment to obtain the following information:

- Personal information, such as age, marital status, job classification, and length of employment
- Chief complaint (in the caller's words)
- Presenting problem(s)
- Nature of the crisis and plan for resolution, if a crisis call
- History bearing on the presenting problem
- Attempted solutions and results
- History of psychiatric treatment
- Mental status information (including assessment of suicide or homicide risk)

This telephone assessment is never intended to supplant or replace an in-depth, confidential, face-to-face psychosocial evaluation with an EAP professional in a private office setting. Instead, it serves the limited but useful purpose of helping the EAP specialist triage callers to appropriate levels of care and practitioners. In complex cases, EAP specialists have the option of seeking advice from colleagues (e.g., another EAP specialist or a supervisor).

Referral to Community Services

If the caller describes problems related to child care, elder care, or financial, legal, or career issues, the EAP specialist usually makes a referral to an appropriate community resource, including (but not limited to) one or more of the following:

- Child or adult day care services
- Home health services
- Consumer credit counseling
- Self-help or twelve-step groups (e.g., Alcoholics Anonymous, Al-Anon, Narcotics Anonymous)
- Legal aid services
- Consumer protection agencies or organizations

21st Century EAP Company also offers enhanced dependent care and legal resources, described separately.

Referral to an EAP Practitioner

If the caller's problem can be resolved by brief assessment and solution-oriented therapy, the caller is referred to a network practitioner who is privileged to deliver EAP services, skilled in treating problems similar to the caller's, and located near the caller's office or home. Individuals who meet 21st Century EAP Company's criteria for EAP referral and services include those who meet the following conditions:

- Not in an active psychiatric crisis (i.e., not in need of inpatient treatment or crisis intervention)
- Not dangerous to self or others
- Not reporting evidence of an active psychotic process
- Not currently in MH/SA treatment
- Assessed as having any of the following *Diagnostic and Statistical Manual* Fourth Edition, V code diagnoses—reflective of problems typically *not* covered by most MH/SA benefit plans but are covered by the EAP:
  —Marital/relationship problem
  —Occupational problem
  —Parent/child problem
  —Uncomplicated bereavement
  —Academic problems
  —Childhood or adolescent antisocial behavior
  —Adult antisocial behavior
  —Borderline intellectual functioning
  —Malingering
  —Noncompliance with medical treatment
  —Other interpersonal problem
  —Other specified family circumstance
  —Phase-of-life problem or other life circumstance problem
  —No diagnosis
- Assessed as having any of the following presenting problems:
  —Physical ailments
  —Financial difficulties
  —Legal issues
  —Life stress situations that cause anxiety, depression, frustration, inadequacy, and loneliness
- Referred by a supervisor

The EAP practitioner develops a plan for resolving the presenting problem(s) and sees the employee or dependent for the number of sessions authorized, not to exceed the contractual benefit. In EAPs offering five or more counseling visits, research substantiates that 60 to 65 percent of EAP-appropriate cases are resolved within the visit limit.

Referral to the MH/SA Benefit

If the EAP specialist determines that longer-term therapy is indicated, as would be the case for individuals with serious psychiatric and/or substance abuse problems, the employee or dependent is referred directly to the MH/SA benefit.

The EAP specialist continues to follow the case through the conclusion of treatment and aftercare, participating actively in treatment planning, inpatient and/or outpatient authorizations, and discharge/aftercare planning.

Care Management Services

21st Century EAP Company's staff of EAP specialists perform a variety of care management services, including the following:

- Initial assessment and referral to a network EAP practitioner
- Concurrent reviews (for short-term treatment EAP models)

Their oversight of the network EAP practitioners enhances the quality of care delivered and ensures that all care delivered is necessary and appropriate.

Once the initial intake has been completed and a practitioner has been selected, the EAP specialist telephones the EAP practitioner and requests that the practitioner contact the employee within forty-eight hours to set up an appointment or that the employee will be contacting the practitioner. If the employee declines to give permission for the practitioner to call back, the EAP specialist asks the employee to call the EAP practitioner directly for an appointment. The EAP specialist then mails pertinent case-related material, such as an authorization letter and EAP Client Satisfaction Questionnaire, to the EAP practitioner.

If the employee has elected to contact the practitioner for an appointment but does not follow through, the practitioner notifies the EAP specialist. The EAP specialist makes further attempts to contact the employee, reassesses the employee's clinical need, and connects the individual with appropriate EAP services.

If after EAP services have been provided by the EAP practitioner, further MH/SA services are indicated, the practitioner and employee develop an appropriate plan for approval by the EAP specialist, if 21st Century EAP Company also manages the customer's behavioral health benefits. If access to MH/SA benefits is recommended by the EAP practitioner, and the specialist concurs with this recommendation, the EAP specialist makes an appropriate referral to the employee's MH/SA benefit.

Final disposition planning occurs when the employee's participation in the EAP is terminated and the episode of EAP care has ended. Thus, direct assistance to an employee is terminated after both the EAP practitioner and the 21st Century EAP Company EAP specialist agree that the EAP episode has been completed, and when the practitioner and employee have discussed whether additional care through community-based services or access to MH/SA benefits is needed. EAP services to the individual then are concluded. Client satisfaction survey results are tabulated and reported to the customer in aggregate form. The EAP practitioner notifies 21st Century EAP Company of the case disposition, and case closing information is also tabulated and reported to the customer in aggregate form, with no EAP client-identifying information included.

Program Promotion Through Supervisor Training and Employee Orientation

EAP utilization is maximized when employees and supervisors fully understand what the EAP has to offer and how services can be easily accessed. 21st Century EAP Company's promotional activities—including supervisor training, employee orientations, and wellness workshops—are all designed to stimulate interest and promote early, appropriate referrals. 21st Century EAP Company works in partnership with the customer to design a promotional program that meets your informational and workplace scheduling needs.

Supervisor Training

Management's understanding, support, and assistance in promoting the EAP is critical to its success. 21st Century EAP Company's management training sessions encourage supervisory referrals to the EAP and communicate the clinical and financial advantages of encouraging wellness and early intervention. During account implementation, we distribute *Supervisor Guides to the EAP* and present supervisory training sessions that address such topics as these:

- EAP overview
- How the EAP works
- EAP services
- Confidentiality of EAP services and limits to confidentiality
- The supervisor's role in employee performance
- Referring an employee to the EAP
- Role of the EAP professional

Employee Orientation Sessions

Customer employees are more motivated to contact the EAP when they fully understand how it works and what it can offer to enhance the quality of their lives. The following communications materials can be distributed:

- Letter of introduction for each employee
- EAP brochure for each employee/household
- Wallet cards

- Posters
- Quarterly newsletter

Wellness Workshops

21st Century EAP Product offers an array of wellness programs and other on-site training opportunities.

Supervisor Consultations

We offer unlimited consultations for supervisors who are dealing with troubled employees. 21st Century EAP Company's EAP specialists will assist your managers in preparing for, and following up on, performance problem interviews with employees.

Critical Incident Stress Debriefings (CISDs)

CISDs are designed to help employees who are directly or indirectly affected by traumatic events in or outside the workplace, such as accidents, natural disasters, robberies, suicides, homicides, and hostage situations. We typically conduct CISDs at the work site and encourage employees to access the EAP for ongoing, stress-related help. 21st Century EAP Company's critical incident team provides group support to all affected employees, as well as individual counseling for those who request it.

Drug-Free Workplace Programs

21st Century EAP Company's staff includes specialists dedicated to the interpretation and implementation of the Drug-Free Workplace Act. Drawing on our extensive substance abuse treatment experience, we work with our clients to establish effective assessment, counseling, and aftercare programs.

Supervisor Referrals to the EAP

Supervisor referrals of employees to the EAP may result from a variety of circumstances. Here are commonly encountered types of supervisory referrals and their definitions:

- *Informal EAP referrals:* A supervisor becomes aware that a problem of some kind has begun to impact an employee's performance, and the supervisor suggests (but does not require) that the employee access EAP services.

- *Formal EAP referrals:* A supervisor has concerns about the performance of an employee and has moved through the progressive discipline process to a point at which the employee's job is at risk and participation in EAP services is recommended.
- *Mandatory referrals:* An employee who participated in a drug test has tested positive, and participation in the EAP is offered as a means by which to assess the nature and extent of the problem. Compliance is strongly recommended and will need to be communicated to the employer for monitoring purposes.

The general process we recommend for establishing return-to-work agreements following a supervisor referral to EAP services is outlined here:

- The supervisor calls the 21st Century EAP Company EAP specialist for a consultation and supplies basic information, such as the employee's name and work and home telephone numbers; reason for the informal, formal, or mandatory referral; and work-related problems leading up to the suspension, if applicable.
- If a referral is made to an EAP network practitioner, the practitioner obtains the following: signed permission from the employee to release confidential information, an appropriate return-to-work agreement, and authorization for the EAP specialist to release treatment progress information to the employer.
- The EAP network practitioner reports progress to the EAP specialist. If the EAP specialist's initial assessment identified the need for an MH/SA referral, the EAP specialist helps to determine an appropriate course of action.
- The EAP network practitioner conducts an assessment and then discusses an individualized treatment plan with the 21st Century EAP Company EAP specialist. When the treatment plan is finalized, it is communicated to the employee.

The EAP specialist initiates aftercare or workplace adjustment planning with the treating practitioner when a member has completed MH/SA treatment but has issues related to a successful return to work. This planning involves determining which EAP services are appropriate to help the member maintain gains made during treatment.

Nationwide EAP Practitioner Network

21st Century EAP Company successfully utilizes a network model to deliver EAP and MH/SA services. When 21st Century EAP Company identifies network needs, we implement recruitment procedures to secure new practitioners who meet specific requirements of client accounts within the defined geographic areas.

EAP Practitioner Credentialing Process

21st Century EAP Company offers a complete multidisciplinary network of professionals: psychiatrists, psychologists, social workers, certified employee assistance professionals (CEAPs), and other master's-level clinicians. All agree to work within our system of managing care, including participating in our quality improvement (QI) activities. 21st Century EAP Company's staff meet the same qualifications and credentialing requirements as our network practitioners; this facilitates better peer monitoring and EAP client matching. Our facility/program network is designed to provide a full continuum of care, ranging from hospital inpatient and residential treatment services to in-home and crisis diversion programs.

Our basic credentialing criteria/standards for all our network practitioners include the following:

1. Current licensure for independent practice in their specialty at the highest level in the state in which they practice.
2. Malpractice insurance coverage (Physician providers must carry minimum malpractice and liability insurance coverage of $1,000,000 per occurrence and $3,000,000 aggregate. Required coverage for other mental health care professionals is $1,000,000 per occurrence and $1,000,000 aggregate).
3. Membership in a national professional association that ascribes to a professional code of ethics (e.g., Employee Assistance Professionals Association, National Association of Social Workers, American Psychiatric Association, American Psychological Association, or American Nursing Association).

21st Century EAP Company conducts a rigorous credentialing process that matches standard industry practices. A four-step process is used to verify and approve the qualifications of practitioners interested in joining our network to serve your employees:

- *Prescreening and completion of application packet:* Practitioners are prescreened by telephone to determine whether they meet minimum criteria for licensure and professional liability coverage. Those who do receive application packets that include criteria for network participation; responsibilities and agreements; and a detailed, formal application that collects information regarding professional competencies, practice history, and areas of specialization.

- *Source verification of credentials:* All information submitted is primary source verified. Any legal actions or sanctions imposed by licensing/certification boards or professional societies are investigated.
- *Approval of credentials and profiling:* Once primary source verification is completed, potential practitioners are asked to provide supplementary information pertaining to clinical specialties, including treatment modalities, client populations served (e.g., children and adolescents, women only), and experience with specific disorders. This information is entered online and incorporated into a practitioner profile that is accessible to our EAP specialists.
- *Recredentialing:* Every two years, practitioners must complete the processes of administrative recredentialing. Administrative recredentialing requires the practitioner to update documentation such as evidence of current licensure and malpractice insurance coverage.

Through our combined credentialing and privileging process, 21st Century EAP Company verifies both general competence and specific proficiency in treating the range of MH/SA diagnoses and conditions. By taking the extra step of privileging, we ensure that care managers refer every patient to a practitioner who has the qualifications and expertise to treat that member's particular behavioral health need. This matching results in fewer episodes of care, fewer outpatient visits or inpatient days per episode of care, and very few repeat referrals to different practitioners for the same presenting condition and patient.

Additional EAP Network Practitioner Credentialing Criteria

All EAP practitioners are licensed clinicians in a human services-related field. In addition, they must meet one of the following criteria if not licensed by their state as an EA professional: four years full-time EAP experience as an EA professional, current license or certification as an addictions counselor or substance abuse counselor at the state or national level, or current CEAP certification.

Complaint Resolution

21st Century EAP Company recognizes the right of each employee and practitioner to a formal mechanism by which to lodge a complaint related to service and quality concerns.

We define a complaint as a written or verbal expression of concern that requires resolution and response. Our response may be verbal or in writing, depending on the nature of the complaint. Complaints may commonly address dissatisfaction with the following:

- Access to service
- Quality of service
- Timeliness of service
- Practitioner or staff attitude or office environment
- Utilization management process or decision
- Inaccurate or inadequate information

Complaints are forwarded to the appropriate area for investigation and resolution, and the nature and outcome of each complaint are trended and reported to the customer.

Face-to-Face Service Delivery Through Our Nationwide Practitioner Network

21st Century EAP Company's credentialed network includes practitioners in all fifty states and Canada. Current practice information about our contracted practitioners is available online to our EAP specialists who serve your employees. All network practitioners are credentialed and recredentialed every two years to deliver services for specific mental health problems and patient populations. Our EAP practitioner recruitment specialists enable us to identify new EA practitioners quickly and efficiently.

Local Account Management

21st Century EAP Company's national office provides support to our local account managers. This support includes services related to clinical policy and procedure development, quality assurance, network development and management, information systems, claims, and program administration.

Reporting to Customers

21st Century EAP Company provides quarterly EAP reports to our customers. Reports include information such as the source of referral (e.g., self, supervisor), demographic information and presenting problems of employees requesting services, and types of referrals made. EAP reports can be used as a basis for gaining a broad concept of employee needs/problems and for planning future preventive health interventions or additional targeted EAP services.

Quality Improvement Services

Through our QI program, 21st Century EAP Company sets and achieves specific performance goals related to quality and service for your account. Evaluation of the data collected from systems reports, case records, and peer reviews provides the basis for planning improvements in services, taking corrective action to address deficiencies, and minimizing risk potential. 21st Century EAP Company's successful QI program has been validated by independent accreditation and review organizations, including the EASNA's EAP Accreditation Program and the NCQA.

21st Century EAP Company's information systems support all of the internal care management functions and incorporate eligibility and benefits information, claims data, and all necessary clinical data at the patient, practitioner, and account levels. We offer standard reporting packages and have the capacity to develop ad hoc and customized utilization, cost, and demographic reports.

CONCLUSION

21st Century EAP Company has the organizational size, depth, and experience to facilitate administration and delivery of services and to help the customer meet its EAP goals. We look forward to working collaboratively with you to provide cost-effective, patient-oriented EAP and care management services.

Appendix C

Magellan Behavioral Health Medical Necessity Criteria, 2000

PREAMBLE

Principles of Certification

Magellan Behavioral Health is committed to the philosophy of providing treatment at the most appropriate, least intensive level of care necessary to provide safe and effective treatment and meet the individual patient's biopsychosocial needs. We see the continuum of care as a fluid treatment pathway, where individuals may enter treatment at any level and be moved to more or less intensive settings or levels of care as their changing clinical needs dictate.

The Magellan Behavioral Health Medical Necessity Criteria guide both providers and reviewers to the most appropriate level of care for a patient. While these criteria will assign the most safe and effective level of care in nearly all instances, an infrequent number of cases may fall beyond their definition and scope. Thorough and careful review of each case, including consultation with supervising clinicians, will identify these exceptions. As in the review of nonexceptional cases, clinical judgment consistent with the standards of good medical practice will be used to resolve these exceptional cases.

Clinical decisions about each case are based on the clinical features of the individual case, the medical necessity criteria, and the real resources available. We recognize that a full array of services is not available everywhere. When a medically necessary level does not exist (e.g., rural locations), we will authorize "individual case management" (support for extracontractual benefits) or a higher than otherwise necessary level of care to ensure that authorizations are made for services that are available and will meet the patient's essential needs for safe and effective treatment.

MEDICAL NECESSITY DEFINITION

Magellan Behavioral Health reviews mental health and substance abuse treatment for medical necessity. Magellan defines medical necessity as:

Services by a provider to identify or treat an illness that has been diagnosed or suspected. They are:
   a. consistent with:
      (1) the diagnosis and treatment of a condition; and
      (2) standards of good medical practice;
   b. required for other than convenience; and
   c. the most appropriate supply or level of service.
When applied to inpatient care, the term means: the needed care can only be safely given on an inpatient basis.

Each criteria set, within each level of care category (see below) is a more detailed elaboration of the above definition for the purposes of establishing medical necessity for these health care services. Each set is characterized by admission and continued stay criteria. The admission criteria are further delineated by severity of need and intensity of service.

Particular rules in each criteria set apply in guiding a provider or reviewer to a medically necessary level of care (please note the possibility and consideration of exceptional cases described in the preamble when these rules may not apply). For admission, both the severity of need and intensity of service criteria must be met. The continued stay of a patient at a particular level of care requires the continued stay criteria to be met. (Note: this often requires that the admission criteria are still fulfilled.) Specific rules for the admission and continued stay groupings are noted within the criteria sets.

LEVELS OF CARE

Magellan Behavioral Health believes that optimal, high-quality care is best delivered when patients receive care that coincides with their needs in the least intensive, least restrictive setting possible. Not only does this philosophy result in the highest quality of care, but also care that is most effective.

Magellan Behavioral Health has defined six levels of care as detailed in the following. These levels of care may be further qualified by the distinct needs of certain populations who frequently require behavioral health services. Children, adolescents, geriatric adults, and those with substance use and eating disorders often have special concerns not present in adults with mental health disorders alone. In particular, special issues related to family involvement, physical symptoms, medical conditions, and social supports may apply. More specific criteria sets in certain of the level of care definitions address these population issues.

The six level of care definitions are:

1. *Hospitalization*—Hospitalization describes the high level of skilled psychiatric and substance abuse services provided in a facility. This could be a free-standing psychiatric hospital, a psychiatric unit of a general hospital, or a detoxification unit in a hospital. Settings that are eligible for this level of care are licensed at the hospital level and provide twenty-four-hour medical and nursing care.

2. *Residential Treatment Center*—Residential Treatment Center is defined as a nonhospital twenty-four-hour inpatient level of care that provides persons with long-term or severe mental disorders, and persons with substance abuse/dependency disorders, with residential care. This care would include treatment with a range of diagnostic and therapeutic behavioral health services that cannot be provided through existing community programs. Residential care will also include training in the basic skills of living as determined necessary for each client. Residential treatment for psychiatric conditions and rehabilitation treatment for alcohol and substance abuse are included in this level of care. Settings that are eligible for this level of care are licensed at the residential intermediate level or as an intermediate care facility (ICF). Licensure requirements for this level of care may vary by state.

3. *Supervised Living*—Supervised Living for substance-related disorders includes community-based residential detoxification programs; community-based residential rehabilitation in halfway and quarterway houses; group homes; specialized foster care homes which serve a limited number of individuals in community-based, home-like settings; and other residential settings which require abstinence (e.g., residences patterned after the Oxford House model).

Supervised Living for mentally ill individuals includes: community residential crisis intervention units; supervised apartments; halfway houses; group homes; foster care that serves a limited number of individuals (e.g., group homes generally serve up to eight; foster care homes generally serve one or two) in community-based, home-like settings; and other residential settings which provide supervision and other specialized custodial services.

This level of care combines outpatient treatment on an individual, group, and/or family basis (usually provided by outside practitioners) with assistance and supervision in managing basic day-to-day activities and responsibilities. These settings are often licensed as halfway houses or group homes depending on the state.

4. *Partial Hospital, Day Treatment, and Twenty-Three-Hour Beds*— These programs are defined as structured and medically supervised day, evening, and/or night treatment programs. Program services are provided at least four hours/day. The services are essentially the same nature and intensity (including medical and nursing) as would be provided in a hospital except that the patient is in the program less than twenty-four hours/day. The patient is not considered a resident at the program. The range of services offered is designed to address a mental health and/or substance-related disorder through an individualized treatment plan provided by a coordinated multidisciplinary treatment team.

5. *Intensive Outpatient Programs*—Intensive outpatient programs are defined as having the capacity for planned, structured, service provision of at least two hours per day or six hours per week. These encounters are usually comprised of coordinated and integrated multidisciplinary services. The range of services offered is designed to address a mental or a substance use disorder and could include group, individual, family, or multifamily group psychotherapy, psychoeducational services, and adjunctive services such as medical monitoring. These services would include multiple or extended treatment/rehabilitation/counseling visits or professional supervision and support. Program models include structured "crisis intervention program," "psychiatric or psychosocial rehabilitation," and some "day treatment." (Although treatment for substance-related disorders typically includes involvement in a self-help program, such as Alcoholics Anonymous or Narcotics Anonymous, program time as described here excludes time spent in these self-help programs, which are offered by community volunteers without charge.)

6. *Outpatient Treatment*—Outpatient treatment is typically individual, family, and/or group psychotherapy and consultative services (including nursing home consultation). Times for provision of these service episodes range from fifteen minutes (i.e., medication check) to fifty minutes (i.e., individual, conjoint, family psychotherapy), and may last up to two hours (e.g., group psychotherapy).

HOSPITALIZATION, PSYCHIATRIC, ADULT

I. Criteria for Admission

All conditions must be met for severity of need and intensity of service to satisfy the criteria for admission.

Severity of Need

Criteria A and either B, C, or D must be met to satisfy the criteria for severity of need.

A. Patient must have a diagnosed or suspected mental illness. Mental illness is defined as a psychiatric disorder that, by accepted medical standards, can be expected to improve significantly through medically necessary and appropriate therapy. Presence of the illness(es) must be documented through the assignment of appropriate DSM-IV codes on all applicable axes (I-V).
B. Patient demonstrates imminent risk for severe self-injury, with an inability to guarantee safety, as manifested by any one of the following:
    1. Recent, serious, and dangerous suicide attempt, indicated by degree of lethal intent, impulsivity, and/or concurrent intoxication, including an inability to plan reliably for safety.
    2. Current suicidal ideation with intent, realistic plan, or available means that is severe and dangerous.
    3. Recent self-mutilation that is dangerous and severely compromises the patient's medical and/or functional status.
    4. Inability to adequately care for own physical needs, through disordered, disorganized, or bizarre behavior, representing potential for imminent serious harm to self.
C. Patient demonstrates imminent risk for severe injury to others as manifested by any of the following:
    1. Active plan, means, and lethal intent to seriously injure others.
    2. Recent assaultive behaviors that indicate a high risk for recurrent and serious injury to others.
    3. Recent and serious physically destructive acts that indicate a high risk for recurrence and serious injury to others.
D. The patient requires an acute psychiatric intervention(s) that will result in a high probability of serious, imminent, and dangerous deterioration of general medical and/or mental health.

Intensity of Service

Criteria A, B, and C must be met to satisfy the criteria for intensity of service.

A. The evaluation and assignment of the mental illness diagnosis must take place in a face-to-face evaluation of the patient performed by an attending physician prior to, or within twenty-four hours following, the admission.

B. This care must require an individual plan of active psychiatric treatment that includes twenty-four-hour need for, and access to, the full spectrum of psychiatric staffing. This psychiatric staffing must provide twenty-four-hour services, including quiet room, seclusion, intermittent restraints, and suicidal/homicidal observation and precautions.

C. A discharge plan is initially formulated that is directly linked to the behaviors and/or symptoms that resulted in admission. This plan receives regular review and revision that includes an appropriate and timely evaluation of posthospitalization needs.

II. Criteria for Continued Stay

Criteria A, B, C, and D and either E, F, or G must be met to satisfy the criteria for continued stay.

A. The admission criteria must continue to be met.

B. The current treatment plan should include documentation of diagnosis (DSM-IV axes I-V), discharge planning, individualized goals of treatment, and treatment modalities needed and provided on a twenty-four-hour basis.

C. The patient's progress confirms that the presenting or newly defined problem(s) will respond to the current treatment plan.

D. There should be daily progress notes documenting the provider's treatment and the patient's response to treatment.

E. Clinical evidence indicates the persistence of the problems that caused the admission to the degree which would necessitate continued hospitalization, despite therapeutic efforts, or the emergence of additional problems consistent with the admission criteria and to the degree which would necessitate continued hospitalization.

F. There is a severe reaction to medication or need for further monitoring and adjustment of dosage in an inpatient setting. This should be documented in daily progress notes by a physician.

G. There is clinical evidence that disposition planning, progressive increases in hospital privileges, and/or attempts at therapeutic reentry into the community have resulted in, or would result in, exacerbation of the psychiatric illness to the degree that would necessitate continued hospitalization.

HOSPITALIZATION, PSYCHIATRIC, CHILD AND ADOLESCENT

I. Criteria for Admission

All conditions must be met for severity of need and intensity of service to satisfy the criteria for admission.

Severity of Need

Criteria A and either B, C, or D must be met to satisfy the criteria for severity of need.

A. Patient must have a diagnosed or suspected mental illness. Mental illness is defined as a psychiatric disorder that, by accepted medical standards, can be expected to improve significantly through medically necessary and appropriate therapy. Presence of the illness(es) must be documented through the assignment of appropriate DSM-IV codes on all applicable axes (I-V).

B. Patient demonstrates imminent risk for severe self-injury, with an inability to guarantee safety, as manifested by any one of the following:
   1. Recent, serious, and dangerous suicide attempt, indicated by degree of lethal intent, impulsivity, and/or concurrent intoxication, including an inability to plan reliably for safety.
   2. Current suicidal ideation with intent, realistic plan, or available means that is severe and dangerous.
   3. Recent self-mutilation that is dangerous and severely compromises the patient's medical and/or functional status.
   4. Inability to adequately care for own physical needs, through disordered, disorganized, or bizarre behavior, representing potential for imminent serious harm to self.

C. Patient demonstrates imminent risk for severe injury to others as manifested by any of the following:
   1. Active plan, means, and lethal intent to seriously injure others.
   2. Recent assaultive behaviors that indicate a high risk for recurrent and serious injury to others.
   3. Recent and serious physically destructive acts that indicate a high risk for recurrence and serious injury to others.

D. The patient requires an acute psychiatric intervention(s) that will result in a high probability of serious, imminent, and dangerous deterioration of general medical and/or mental health.

Intensity of Service

Criteria A, B, and C must be met to satisfy the criteria for intensity of service.

A. The evaluation and assignment of the mental illness diagnosis must take place in a face-to-face evaluation of the patient performed by an attending physician prior to, or within twenty-four hours following, the admission.
B. This care must require an individual plan of active psychiatric treatment that includes twenty-four-hour need for, and access to, the full spectrum of psychiatric staffing. This psychiatric staffing must provide twenty-four-hour services, including quiet room, seclusion, intermittent restraints, and suicidal/homicidal observation and precautions.
C. A discharge plan is initially formulated that is directly linked to the behaviors and/or symptoms that resulted in admission. This plan receives regular review and revision that includes as appropriate and timely evaluation of posthospitalization needs.

II. Criteria for Continued Stay

Criteria A, B, C, D, and E and either F, G, or H must be met to satisfy the criteria for continued stay.

A. The admission criteria must continue to be met.
B. The current treatment plan should include documentation of diagnosis (DSM-IV axes I-V), discharge planning, individualized goals of treatment, and treatment modalities needed and provided on a twenty-four-hour basis.
C. The patient's progress confirms that the presenting or newly defined problem(s) will respond to the current treatment plan.
D. There should be daily progress notes documenting the provider's treatment and the patient's response to treatment.
E. There should be evidence of intensive family involvement occurring several times per week unless the treatment plan specifically indicates a clinical need for less frequent involvement.
F. Clinical evidence indicates the persistence of the problems that caused the admission to the degree which would necessitate continued hospitalization, despite therapeutic efforts, or the emergence of additional problems consistent with the admission criteria and to the degree which would necessitate continued hospitalization.

G. There is a severe reaction to medication or need for further monitoring and adjustment of dosage in an inpatient setting. This should be documented in daily progress notes by a physician.
H. There is clinical evidence that disposition planning, progressive increases in hospital privileges, and/or attempts at therapeutic reentry into the community have resulted in, or would result in, exacerbation of the psychiatric illness to the degree that would necessitate continued hospitalization.

HOSPITALIZATION, PSYCHIATRIC, GERIATRIC

I. Criteria for Admission

All conditions must be met for severity of need and intensity of service to satisfy the criteria for admission.

Severity of Need

Criteria A and either B, C, or D must be met to satisfy the criteria for severity of need.

A. Patient must have a diagnosed or suspected mental illness. Mental illness is defined as a psychiatric disorder that, by accepted medical standards, can be expected to improve significantly through medically necessary and appropriate therapy. Presence of the illness(es) must be documented through the assignment of appropriate DSM-IV codes on all applicable axes (I-V).
B. Patient demonstrates imminent risk for severe self-injury, with an inability to guarantee safety, as manifested by any one of the following:
    1. Recent, serious, and dangerous suicide attempt, indicated by degree of lethal intent, impulsivity, and/or concurrent intoxication, including an inability to plan reliably for safety.
    2. Current suicidal ideation with intent, realistic plan, or available means that is severe and dangerous.
    3. Recent self-mutilation that is dangerous and severely compromises the patient's medical and/or functional status.
    4. Inability to adequately care for own physical needs, through disordered, disorganized, or bizarre behavior, representing potential for imminent serious harm to self.
C. Patient demonstrates imminent risk for severe injury to others as manifested by any of the following:

1. Active plan, means, and lethal intent to seriously injure others.
2. Recent assaultive behaviors that indicate a high risk for recurrent and serious injury to others.
3. Recent and serious physically destructive acts that indicate a high risk for recurrence and serious injury to others.

D. The patient requires an acute psychiatric intervention(s) that will result in a high probability of serious, imminent, and dangerous deterioration of general medical and/or mental health.

Intensity of Service

Criteria A, B, C, and D must be met to satisfy the criteria for intensity of service.

A. The evaluation and assignment of the mental illness diagnosis must take place in a face-to-face evaluation of the patient performed by an attending physician prior to, or within twenty-four hours following, the admission.
B. This care must require an individual plan of active psychiatric treatment that includes twenty-four-hour need for, and access to, the full spectrum of psychiatric staffing. In addition to skilled nursing care for activities of daily living and supervision required for structure and redirection of behavior, the psychiatric staffing must provide twenty-four-hour services, including quiet room, seclusion, intermittent restraints, and suicidal/homicidal observation and precautions.
C. For those patients whose comorbid medical conditions may contribute to their mental status, there must be the availability of an appropriate initial medical assessment and ongoing medical management.
D. A discharge plan is initially formulated that is directly linked to the behaviors and/or symptoms that resulted in admission. This plan receives regular review and revision that includes as appropriate and timely evaluation of posthospitalization needs.

II. Criteria for Continued Stay

Criteria A, B, C, D, and E and either F, G, or H must be met to satisfy the criteria for continued stay.

A. The admission criteria must continue to be met.
B. The current treatment plan should include documentation of diagnosis (DSM-IV axes I-V), discharge planning, individualized goals of treat-

ment and treatment modalities needed and provided on a twenty-four-hour basis.

C. The patient's progress confirms that the presenting or newly defined problem(s) will respond to the current treatment plan.

D. There should be daily progress notes documenting the provider's treatment and the patient's response to treatment.

E. There should be evidence that disposition planning includes ongoing contact with facility of residence, personal caretakers, and medical caretakers.

F. Clinical evidence indicates the persistence of the problems that caused the admission to the degree which would necessitate continued hospitalization, despite therapeutic efforts, or the emergence of additional problems consistent with the admission criteria and to the degree which would necessitate continued hospitalization.

G. There is a severe reaction to medication or need for further monitoring and adjustment of dosage in an inpatient setting. This should be documented in daily progress notes by a physician.

H. There is clinical evidence that disposition planning, progressive increases in hospital privileges, and/or attempts at therapeutic reentry into the community have resulted in or would result in, exacerbation of the psychiatric illness to the degree that would necessitate continued hospitalization.

HOSPITALIZATION, EATING DISORDERS

I. Criteria for Admission

All conditions must be met for severity of need and intensity of service to satisfy the criteria for admission.

Severity of Need

Criteria A and one of criteria B, C, D, or E must be met to satisfy the criteria for severity of need.

A. Patients must have a *primary* diagnosis of Anorexia Nervosa, Bulimia Nervosa, or Eating Disorder Not Otherwise Specified. The illness can be expected to improve significantly through medically necessary and appropriate therapy, by accepted medical standards. Patients hospitalized because of another primary psychiatric disorder who have a coexisting eating disorder should be reviewed according to the criteria below *only* if the primary psychiatric disorder no longer requires hospitalization.

B. Body weight less than 75 percent of Ideal Body Weight (IBW) or Body Mass Index (BMI) of 18 or below. If body weight is greater than 75 percent of IBW (or BMI > 18), this criterion can be met if there is evidence of weight loss of >15 percent in one month or weight loss associated with physiologic instability unexplained by any other medical condition. This criterion may be satisfied in children and adolescents who have body weight less than 85 percent of that expected during a period of growth.

C. Medical consequences of the eating-disordered behavior that present the potential for imminent harm such that immediate medical and psychiatric stabilization is necessary before ambulatory or residential management can be considered safe or effective. Such medical consequences would include severe malnutrition, emaciation, significant electrolyte or fluid imbalance, cardiac arrhythmias, hypertension, impaired renal function, intestinal atony or obstruction, pancreatitis, gastric dilatation, esophagitis or esophageal tears, and colitis.

D. In bulimia, immediate interruption of the binge-purge cycle is required to avoid imminent, serious harm, due to the presence of a comorbid medical or psychiatric condition (e.g., pregnancy, uncontrolled diabetes, severe depression with suicidal ideation, etc.), with the need to ensure adequate nutrition and absorption of pharmaceuticals.

E. Failure to respond to an adequate therapeutic trial of treatment in a less restrictive setting (residential or partial hospital). An adequate therapeutic trial would, at a minimum, consist of treatment several times per week with twice weekly individual and/or family therapy, either professional group therapy or self-help group involvement, nutritional counseling, and medication if indicated. To meet this criterion, the patient must have significant weight loss (<85 percent IBW), significant impairment in social or occupational functioning, and be uncooperative with treatment (or cooperative only in a highly structured environment) despite having insight and motivation to recover. If patient has failed to improve in an acute residential program, there must be evidence to suggest that necessary changes in the treatment plan cannot be implemented in a residential setting or that inpatient hospitalization is required due to medical comorbidity or need for special feeding.

Intensity of Service

Criteria A, B, and C must be met to satisfy the criteria for intensity of service.

A. The evaluation and assignment of the mental illness diagnosis must take place in a face-to-face evaluation of the patient performed by an attending physician prior to, or within twenty-four hours following, the admission.

B. This care must require an individual plan of active psychiatric treatment that includes twenty-four-hour need for, and access to, the full spectrum of psychiatric staffing. This psychiatric staffing must provide twenty-four-hour services, including quiet room, seclusion, intermittent restraints, and suicidal/homicidal observation and precautions.

C. A discharge plan is initially formulated that is directly linked to the behaviors and/or symptoms that resulted in admission. This plan receives regular review and revision that includes as appropriate and timely evaluation of posthospitalization needs.

II. Criteria for Continued Stay

Criteria A, B, C, D, and E and either F, G, H, I, or J must be met to satisfy the criteria for continued stay.

A. The admission criteria must continue to be met.

B. The current treatment plan should include documentation of diagnosis (DSM-IV axes I-V), discharge planning, individualized goals of treatment, and treatment modalities needed and provided on a twenty-four-hour basis.

C. The patient's progress confirms that the presenting or newly defined problem(s) will respond to the current treatment plan.

D. There should be daily progress notes documenting the provider's treatment and the patient's response to treatment.

E. There should be evidence of intensive family involvement occurring several times per week unless the treatment plan specifically indicates a clinical need for less frequent involvement.

F. The patient's weight remains >85 percent of IBW and he/she fails to achieve a reasonable and expected weight gain despite provision of adequate caloric intake.

G. Continued inability to adhere to a meal plan and maintain control over urges to binge/purge such that continued supervision during and after meals and/or in bathrooms is required. In order to satisfy this criterion, there must be evidence that patient is unable to participate in ambulatory or residential treatment, lacks significant insight into the symptoms of his/her illness, *and* has regressed in response to progressive increases in privilege level.

H. The patient continues to meet Admission Criteria, Severity of Need-C with the need for ongoing medical monitoring of medical consequences of the eating disorder.
I. There is a severe reaction to medication or need for further monitoring and adjustment of dosage in an inpatient setting. This should be documented in daily progress notes by a physician.
J. There is clinical evidence that disposition planning, progressive increases in hospital privileges, and/or attempts at therapeutic reentry into the community have resulted in, or would result in, exacerbation of the psychiatric illness to the degree that would necessitate continued hospitalization.

HOSPITALIZATION, ALCOHOL/DRUG DETOXIFICATION

I. Criteria for Admission

All conditions must be met for severity of need and intensity of service to satisfy the criteria for admission.[1]

Severity of Need

Both Criteria A and B must be met to satisfy the criteria for severity of need.

A. Patient has a history of heavy and continuous alcohol/drug use requiring detoxification services where:
    1. There is either the potential for serious physical harm from the side effects of withdrawal or there are serious medical conditions that complicate the management of withdrawal and in combination with withdrawal endanger the patient's life, *and*
    2. These services cannot be provided on an outpatient basis.
B. Patient presents with signs and symptoms of impending withdrawal and/or a history of complicated withdrawal that endangered the patient's life; seizures; or delirium tremens.

Intensity of Service

Criteria A, B, and C must be met to satisfy the criteria for intensity of service.

A. The evaluation and assignment of the diagnosis must take place in a face-to-face evaluation of the patient performed by an attending physician prior to, or within twenty-four hours following, the admission.
B. This care must require an individual plan of active medical treatment that includes twenty-four-hour need for, and access to, the full spectrum of physician and nurse staffing. This staffing must provide twenty-four-hour services, including skilled observation and medication administration.
C. A discharge plan is initially formulated that is directly linked to the behaviors and/or symptoms that resulted in admission. This plan receives regular review and revision that includes as appropriate and timely evaluation of posthospitalization needs.

II. Criteria for Continued Stay

Criteria A, B, and C must be met to satisfy the criteria for continued stay.

A. All admission criteria are met on a continuing basis.
B. Clinical evidence indicates the need for skilled observation and medical treatment that includes vital sign monitoring every two hours and medication assessments/adjustments.
C. Physical signs and symptoms of acute withdrawal which require intensive nursing and medical treatment intervention on a twenty-four-hour basis. Documentation of this must be noted three times daily, of which one such notation must be made by a physician.

HOSPITALIZATION, COEXISTING PSYCHIATRIC AND SUBSTANCE-RELATED DISORDERS

I. Criteria for Admission

All conditions must be met for severity of need and intensity of service to satisfy the criteria for admission.

Severity of Need

Criteria A and either B, C, or D must be met to satisfy the criteria for severity of need.

A. Patient must have both a diagnosed (or suspected) mental and substance abuse/dependency illness. These illnesses are defined as behavioral disorders that, by accepted medical standards, can be expected to improve significantly through medically necessary and appropriate therapy. Presence of the illnesses must be documented through the assignment of appropriate DSM-IV codes on all applicable axes (I-V).
B. Patient demonstrates imminent risk for severe self-injury, with an inability to guarantee safety, as manifested by any one of the following:
   1. Recent, serious, and dangerous suicide attempt, indicated by degree of lethal intent, impulsivity, and/or concurrent intoxication, including an inability to plan reliably for safety.
   2. Current suicidal ideation with intent, realistic plan, or available means that is severe and dangerous.
   3. Recent self-mutilation that is dangerous and severely compromises the patient's medical and/or functional status.
   4. Inability to adequately care for own physical needs, through disordered, disorganized, or bizarre behavior, representing potential for imminent serious harm to self.
C. Patient demonstrates imminent risk for severe injury to others as manifested by any of the following:
   1. Active plan, means, and lethal intent to seriously injure others.
   2. Recent assaultive behaviors that indicate a high risk for recurrent and serious injury to others.
   3. Recent and serious physically destructive acts that indicate a high risk for recurrence and serious injury to others.
D. The patient requires an acute psychiatric intervention(s) that will result in a high probability of serious, imminent, and dangerous deterioration of general medical and/or mental health.

Intensity of Service

Criteria A, B, and C must be met to satisfy the criteria for intensity of service.

A. The evaluation and assignment of the behavioral illness diagnoses must take place in a face-to-face evaluation of the patient performed by an attending physician prior to, or within twenty-four hours following, the admission.
B. This care must require an individual plan of active psychiatric and substance abuse/dependency treatment that includes twenty-four-hour need for, and access to, the full spectrum of behavioral health staffing (physicians, nurses, counselors, social workers, and other therapists). This

staffing must provide twenty-four-hour services, including quiet room, seclusion, intermittent restraints, and suicidal/homicidal observation and precautions.
C. A discharge plan is initially formulated that is directly linked to the behaviors and/or symptoms that resulted in admission. This plan receives regular review and revision that includes as appropriate and timely evaluation of posthospitalization needs.

II. Criteria for Continued Stay

Criteria A, B, C, D, and E and either F, G, or H must be met to satisfy the criteria for continued stay.

A. The admission criteria must continue to be met.
B. The current treatment plan should include documentation of diagnosis (DSM-IV axes I-V), discharge planning, individualized goals of treatment, and treatment modalities needed and provided on a twenty-four-hour basis.
C. The patient's progress confirms that the presenting or newly defined problem(s) will respond to the current treatment plan.
D. There should be daily progress notes documenting the provider's treatment and the patient's response to treatment.
E. There should be evidence of intensive family involvement occurring several times per week unless the treatment plan specifically indicates a clinical need for less frequent involvement (for child or adolescent patients).
F. Clinical evidence indicates the persistence of the problems that caused the admission to the degree which would necessitate continued hospitalization, despite therapeutic efforts, or the emergence of additional problems consistent with the admission criteria and to the degree which would necessitate continued hospitalization.
G. There is a severe reaction to medication or need for further monitoring and adjustment of dosage in an inpatient setting. This should be documented in daily progress notes by a physician.
H. There is clinical evidence that disposition planning, progressive increases in hospital privileges, and/or attempts at therapeutic reentry into the community have resulted in, or would result in, exacerbation of the psychiatric illness to the degree that would necessitate continued hospitalization.

HOSPITALIZATION, COEXISTING BIOMEDICAL
AND SUBSTANCE-RELATED DISORDERS

I. Criteria for Admission

All conditions must be met for severity of need and intensity of service to satisfy the criteria for admission.[2]

Severity of Need

Criteria A and B must be met to satisfy the criteria for severity of need.

A. Patient must have a diagnosed (or suspected) substance abuse/dependency and biomedical illness. A substance abuse/dependency illness is defined as a behavioral disorder that, by accepted medical standards, can be expected to improve significantly through medically necessary and appropriate therapy. Presence of the substance abuse/dependency illness(es) must be documented through the assignment of appropriate DSM-IV codes on all applicable axes (I-V).
A biomedical illness is a disorder that, by accepted medical standards, can be expected to improve significantly through medically necessary and appropriate therapy. Presence of the biomedical illness(es) must be documented through the assignment of appropriate ICD-9 codes.
B. Patient has a serious biomedical condition that complicates the management of his/her substance abuse/dependency illness. This biomedical condition has the potential to endanger the patient's life or cause serious physical harm.

Intensity of Service

Criteria A, B, C, and D must be met to satisfy the criteria for intensity of service.

A. The evaluation and assignment of the substance abuse/dependency and biomedical diagnosis must take place in a face-to-face evaluation of the patient performed by an attending physician prior to, or within twenty-four hours following, the admission.
B. This care must require an individual plan of active substance abuse/dependency treatment that includes twenty-four-hour need for, and access to, the full spectrum of behavioral health staffing (physicians, nurses, counselors, social workers, and other therapists). This staffing must provide twenty-four-hour services, including quiet room, seclusion, intermittent restraints, and suicidal/homicidal observation and precautions.

C. The biomedical illness(es) requires twenty-four-hour medical monitoring and medical/nursing care which inhibits the patient's ability to be treated in a less intensive setting.

D. A discharge plan is initially formulated that is directly linked to the substance abuse/dependency behaviors/symptoms and biomedical symptoms that resulted in admission. This plan receives regular review and revision that includes an appropriate and timely evaluation of posthospitalization needs.

II. Criteria for Continued Stay

Criteria A, B, C, D, E, and F and either G, H, or I must be met to satisfy the criteria for continued stay.

A. The admission criteria must continue to be met.

B. The current treatment plan should include documentation of diagnosis (DSM-IV axes I-V and ICD-9), discharge planning, individualized goals of treatment, and treatment modalities needed and provided on a twenty-four-hour basis.

C. The patient's progress confirms that the presenting or newly defined problem(s) will respond to the current treatment plan.

D. Clinical evidence indicates the need for twenty-four-hour skilled observation and medical treatment that includes frequent medical monitoring and medication assessments/adjustments.

E. There should be daily progress notes documenting the physician's treatment and the patient's response to treatment.

F. There should be evidence of intensive family involvement occurring several times per week unless the treatment plan specifically indicates a clinical need for less frequent involvement (for child and adolescent patients).

G. Clinical evidence indicates the persistence of the problems that caused the admission to the degree which would necessitate continued hospitalization, despite therapeutic efforts, or the emergence of additional problems consistent with the admission criteria and to the degree which would necessitate continued hospitalization.

H. There is a severe reaction to medication or need for further monitoring and adjustment of dosage in an inpatient setting. This should be documented in daily progress notes by a physician.

I. There is clinical evidence that disposition planning, progressive increases in hospital privileges, and/or attempts at therapeutic reentry into the community have resulted in, or would result in, exacerbation of the substance abuse/dependency or biomedical illness to the degree that would necessitate continued hospitalization.

RESIDENTIAL TREATMENT CENTER (RTC), PSYCHIATRIC, ADULT

I. Criteria for Admission

All conditions must be met for severity of need and intensity of service to satisfy the criteria for admission.

Severity of Need

Criteria A, B, and C must be met to satisfy the criteria for severity of need.

A. There must be clinical evidence that the patient has a long-term and/or severe DSM-IV disorder that has a high degree of potential for leading to acute psychiatric hospitalization in the absence of residential treatment.
B. Due to the psychiatric disorder, the patient exhibits an inability to adequately care for his/her own physical needs. The family and/or other noninpatient community support systems are unable to supply those needs, representing potential serious harm to self or others.
C. The patient's current living environment does not provide the support and access to therapeutic services necessary for recovery.

Intensity of Service

Criteria A, B, and C must be met to satisfy the criteria for intensity of service.

A. The patient must have a psychiatric disorder as defined by DSM-IV that is amenable to active psychiatric treatment. The evaluation and assignment of a diagnosis must result from a face-to-face psychiatric evaluation.
B. The patient requires supervision seven days per week/twenty-four hours per day to develop skills necessary for daily living, to assist with planning and arranging access to a range of educational, therapeutic, and aftercare services, and to develop the adaptive and functional behavior that will allow the patient to live outside of a residential setting.

C. An individualized plan of active psychiatric treatment and residential living support is required. This plan must include evaluation for individual and/or family treatment. This plan must include weekly family and/or supportive person involvement or identify valid reasons why such a plan is not clinically appropriate.

II. Criteria for Continued Stay

Criteria A, B, C, D, E, and F must be met to satisfy the criteria for continued stay.

A. All admission criteria are met on a continuing basis.
B. Clinical evidence of diagnosis and individualized goals of environmental living support provided.
C. Evidence of the need for continued support twenty-four hours per day through a therapeutic living situation.
D. Clinical evidence of therapeutic goals that must be met before the individual can return to a new or previous living situation. There should be evidence that attempts are being made to secure housing in anticipation of this event.
E. Evidence of coordination and access to active psychiatric treatment and services directed at the alleviation of psychiatric symptoms that are interfering with the patient's ability to return to a less intensive level of care.
F. The patient's progress confirms that the presenting or newly defined problem(s) will respond to the current treatment plan.

RESIDENTIAL TREATMENT CENTER (RTC), PSYCHIATRIC, CHILD AND ADOLESCENT

I. Criteria for Admission

All conditions must be met for severity of need and intensity of service to satisfy the criteria for admission.

Severity of Need

Criteria A, B, and C must be met to satisfy the criteria for severity of need.

A. There must be clinical evidence that the child or adolescent has a long-term and/or severe DSM-IV disorder that has a high degree of potential for leading to acute psychiatric hospitalization in the absence of residential inpatient services.
B. Due to the psychiatric disorder, the child or adolescent exhibits an inability to adequately care for his/her own physical needs without external support beyond the family or other noninpatient community support system, representing potential serious harm to self or others.
C. The child or adolescent's current living environment does not provide the support and access to therapeutic services necessary for recovery.

Intensity of Service

Criteria A, B, and C must be met to satisfy the criteria for intensity of service.

A. The child must have a psychiatric disorder that is amenable to active psychiatric treatment. The evaluation and assignment of a DSM-IV diagnosis must result from a face-to-face psychiatric evaluation.
B. The patient requires supervision seven days per week/twenty-four hours per day to develop skills necessary for daily living, to assist with planning and arranging access to a range of educational, therapeutic, and aftercare services, and to develop the adaptive and functional behavior that will allow the patient to live outside of a residential setting.
C. An individual plan of active psychiatric treatment and residential living support is required. This plan must include weekly family and/or supportive person involvement or identify valid reasons why such a plan is not clinically appropriate.

II. Criteria for Continued Stay

Criteria A, B, C, D, E, and F must be met to satisfy the criteria for continued stay.

A. All admission criteria are met on a continuing basis.
B. Clinical evidence of diagnosis and individualized goals of environmental living support provided.
C. Evidence of the need for continued support twenty-four hours per day through a therapeutic living situation.
D. Clinical evidence of therapeutic goals that must be met before the individual can return to a new or previous living situation or, in the case of an eighteen-year-old, make the transition to housing and individual

plans to accomplish these goals. In the latter event, there should be evidence that attempts are being made to secure housing in anticipation of this event.

E. Evidence of coordination and access to active psychiatric treatment and services directed at the alleviation of psychiatric symptoms that are interfering with the patient's ability to return to a less intensive level of care.

F. The patient's progress confirms that the presenting or newly defined problem(s) will respond to the current treatment plan.

RESIDENTIAL TREATMENT CENTER (RTC), SUBSTANCE-RELATED DISORDER, ADULT

I. Criteria for Admission

All conditions must be met for severity of need and intensity of service to satisfy the criteria for admission.

Severity of Need

Criteria A, B, C, and D must be met to satisfy the criteria for severity of need.

A. The patient must have a substance abuse/dependency disorder as defined by DSM-IV that is amenable to active behavioral health treatment.

B. The patient is sufficiently mentally competent and cognitively stable to benefit from admission to an RTC program.

C. Any one of the following must be met to satisfy criterion B:

1. The individual exhibits a pattern of severe alcohol and/or drug abuse as evidenced by significant impairment in social, familial, scholastic, or occupational functioning. Despite recent (i.e., the past three months), appropriate, professional outpatient intervention and sufficient motivation and insight, the patient is continually unable to maintain abstinence and recovery; or

2. The patient is residing in a severely dysfunctional living environment which would undermine effective outpatient treatment; or

3. There is evidence for, or clear and reasonable inference of, serious, imminent physical harm to self or others directly attributable to the continued abuse of substances, which would prohibit treatment in an outpatient setting.

D. For individuals with a history of repeated relapses and a treatment history involving multiple treatment attempts, there must be evidence of the restorative potential for the proposed admission.

Intensity of Service

Criteria A, B, C, and D must be met to satisfy the criteria for intensity of service.

A. The patient must have a substance abuse/dependency disorder as defined by DSM-IV that is amenable to active behavioral health treatment. The evaluation and assignment of a diagnosis must result from a face-to-face behavioral health evaluation.
B. The patient requires supervision seven days per week/twenty-four hours per day to develop skills necessary for daily living, to assist with planning and arranging access to a range of educational, therapeutic, and aftercare services, and to develop the adaptive and functional behavior that will allow the patient to live outside of a residential setting.
C. An individualized plan of active behavioral health treatment and residential living support is required. This plan must include intensive individual, group, and family education and therapy in an inpatient rehabilitative setting. In addition, the plan must include weekly family and/or supportive person involvement or identify valid reasons why such a plan is not clinically appropriate.
D. A discharge plan is initially formulated that is directly linked to the behaviors and/or symptoms that resulted in admission. This plan receives regular review and revision that includes as appropriate and timely evaluation of posthospitalization needs.

II. Criteria for Continued Stay

Criteria A, B, C, and D must be met to satisfy the criteria for continued stay.

A. All admission criteria are met on a continuing basis.
B. There must be documentation at least three times per week supporting the need for continued inpatient treatment. These progress notes should document the providers' treatment and the patient's response to treatment.
C. The persistence of the problems that necessitated the admission to the degree that would necessitate continued inpatient care, despite therapeutic efforts, or the emergence of additional problems consistent with the admission criteria and to the degree that would necessitate continued inpatient care.

D. Clear and reasonable evidence that reentry into the community would result in exacerbation of the illness to the degree that would require an inpatient level of care.

RESIDENTIAL TREATMENT CENTER (RTC), SUBSTANCE-RELATED DISORDER, CHILD AND ADOLESCENT

I. Criteria for Admission

All conditions must be met for severity of need and intensity of service to satisfy the criteria for admission.

Severity of Need

Criteria A, B, C, and D must be met to satisfy the criteria for severity of need.

A. The patient must have a substance abuse/dependency disorder as defined by DSM-IV that is amenable to active behavioral health treatment.
B. The patient is sufficiently mentally competent and cognitively stable to benefit from admission to an RTC program.
C. Any one of the following must be met to satisfy criterion B:
   1. The individual exhibits a pattern of severe alcohol and/or drug abuse as evidenced by significant impairment in social, familial, scholastic, or occupational functioning. Despite recent (i.e., the past three months), appropriate, professional outpatient intervention and sufficient motivation and insight, the patient is continually unable to maintain abstinence and recovery; or
   2. The patient is residing in a severely dysfunctional living environment which would undermine effective outpatient treatment; or
   3. There is actual evidence for, or clear and reasonable inference of, serious, imminent physical harm to self or others directly attributable to the continued abuse of substances, which would prohibit treatment in an outpatient setting.
D. For individuals with a history of repeated relapses and a treatment history involving multiple treatment attempts, there must be evidence of the restorative potential for the proposed admission.

Intensity of Service

Criteria A, B, C, and D must be met to satisfy the criteria for intensity of service.

A. The evaluation and assignment of a diagnosis must result from a face-to-face behavioral health evaluation.
B. The patient requires supervision seven days per week/twenty-four hours per day to develop skills necessary for daily living, to assist with planning and arranging access to a range of educational, therapeutic, and aftercare services, and to develop the adaptive and functional behavior that will allow the patient to live outside of a residential setting.
C. An individualized plan of active behavioral health treatment and residential living support is required. This plan must include intensive individual, group, and family education and therapy in an inpatient rehabilitative setting. In addition, the plan must include weekly family and/or supportive person involvement or identify valid reasons why such a plan is not clinically appropriate.
D. A discharge plan is initially formulated that is directly linked to the behaviors and/or symptoms that resulted in admission. This plan receives regular review and revision that includes as appropriate and timely evaluation of posthospitalization needs.

II. Criteria for Continued Stay

Criteria A, B, C, D, and E must be met to satisfy the criteria for continued stay.

A. All admission criteria are met on a continuing basis.
B. There must be documentation at least three times per week supporting the need for continued inpatient treatment. These progress notes should document the providers' treatment and the patient's response to treatment.
C. The persistence of the problems that necessitated the admission to the degree that would necessitate continued inpatient care, despite therapeutic efforts, or the emergence of additional problems consistent with the admission criteria and to the degree that would necessitate continued inpatient care.
D. Clear and reasonable evidence that reentry into the community would result in exacerbation of the illness to the degree that would require an inpatient level of care.
E. The individual plan of active treatment includes at least weekly family involvement or identified valid reasons why such a plan is not clinically appropriate.

SUPERVISED LIVING, PSYCHIATRIC, ADULT

I. Criteria for Admission

All conditions must be met for severity of need and intensity of service to satisfy the criteria for admission.

Severity of Need

Criteria A, B, C, and D must be met to satisfy the criteria for severity of need.

A. The individual has a primary DSM-IV diagnosis of a mental illness which is the cause of significant functional and psychosocial impairment, and the individual's clinical condition can be expected to be stabilized through the provision of medically necessary supervised residential services in conjunction with medically necessary treatment, rehabilitation, and support.

B. The individual requires supervision and active support to ensure the adequate, effective coping skills necessary to live safely in the community, participate in self-care and treatment, and manage the effects of his/her illness. As a result of the individual's clinical condition (impaired judgment, behavior control, or role functioning, there is significant current risk of one of the following:
   1. Hospitalization or other inpatient care as evidenced by the current course of illness or by the past history of illness; or
   2. Harm to self or others as a result of the mental illness and as evidenced by the current behavior or by the past history.

C. The individual's own resources and social support system are not adequate to provide the level of residential support and supervision currently needed as evidenced by one of the following:
   1. The individual has no residence and no social support; or
   2. The individual has a current residential placement, but the existing placement does not provide sufficiently adequate supervision to ensure safety and participation in treatment; or
   3. The individual has a current residential placement, but the individual is unable to use the relationships in the existing residence to ensure safety and participation in treatment, or the relationships are dysfunctional and undermine the stability of treatment.

D. The individual is judged to be able to reliably cooperate with the rules and supervision provided and to reliably plan for safety in the supervised residence.

Intensity of Service

Criteria A and B must be met to satisfy the criteria for intensity of service.

A. Supervised living for adults will provide supervision and support in a residence outside of the individual's own home and provides needed resources and support not sufficiently available within the individual's own existing social support system. Clinical intervention services, including behavioral, psychological, and psychosocial therapeutic interventions, may also be provided within supervised residential settings, in lieu of or in addition to outpatient and other community-based mental health services.

B. At least one responsible staff person must be present or available by telephone at all times when there are clients on the premises.

II. Criteria for Continued Stay

Criteria A, B, and C must be met to satisfy the criteria for continued stay.

A. The individual continues to have significant functional impairment as a result of a mental illness and the problems that caused the admission persist to the degree that continued placement in a supervised residence is necessary.

B. There continues to be a risk of one of the following:
1. Inpatient admission; or
2. Harm to self or others.

C. There is evidence that the resources and social support system which are available to the individual outside the supervised residence continue to be inadequate to provide the level of residential support and supervision currently needed for safety, self-care, or effective treatment despite current treatment, rehabilitation, and discharge/disposition planning.

SUPERVISED LIVING, SUBSTANCE-RELATED DISORDER, ADULT

I. Criteria for Admission

All conditions must be met for severity of need and intensity of service to satisfy the criteria for admission.

Severity of Need

Criteria A, B, C, and D must be met to satisfy the criteria for severity of need.

A. The individual has a primary DSM-IV diagnosis of a substance-related disorder which is the cause of significant functional and psychosocial impairment, and the individual's clinical condition can be expected to be stabilized through the provision of medically necessary supervised residential services in conjunction with medically necessary treatment, rehabilitation, and support.
B. The individual requires supervision and active support to ensure the adequate, effective coping skills necessary to live safely in the community, participate in self-care and treatment, and manage the effects of his/her disorder. As a result of the individual's clinical condition (impaired judgment, behavior control, or role functioning), there is significant current risk of one of the following:
   1. Hospitalization or other inpatient care as evidenced by the current clinical course or by the past clinical history; or
   2. Harm to self or others as a result of the substance-related disorder as evidenced by the current behavior or by the past history.
C. The individual's own resources and social support system are not adequate to provide the level of residential support and supervision currently needed as evidenced by one of the following:
   1. The individual has no residence and no social support; or
   2. The individual has a current residential placement, but the existing placement does not provide sufficiently adequate supervision to ensure safety and participation in treatment; or
   3. The individual has a current residential placement, but the individual is unable to use the relationships in the existing residence to ensure safety and participation in treatment, or the relationships are dysfunctional and undermine the stability of treatment.
D. The individual is judged to be medically stable, able to reliably cooperate with the rules and supervision provided, and able to reliably plan for safety in the supervised residence.

Intensity of Service

Criteria A and B must be met to satisfy the criteria for intensity of service.

A. Supervised living for substance-related disorders will provide supervision and support for individuals with such problems. Clinical intervention

services, including psychological and psychosocial therapeutic interventions, may also be provided within supervised residential settings, in lieu of or in addition to outpatient and other community-based services.
B. At least one responsible staff person must be present or available by telephone at all times when there are clients on the premises.

II. Criteria for Continued Stay

Criteria A, B, and C must be met to satisfy the criteria for continued stay.

A. The individual continues to have significant functional impairment as a result of the substance-related disorder and the problems that caused the admission persist to the degree that continued placement in a supervised residence is necessary.
B. There continues to be a risk of one of the following:
    1. Inpatient admission; or
    2. Harm to self or others.
C. There is evidence that the resources and social support system which are available to the individual outside the supervised residence continue to be inadequate to provide the level of residential support and supervision currently needed to promote recovery and for safety, self-care, or effective treatment despite current treatment, rehabilitation, and discharge/disposition planning.

SUPERVISED LIVING, PSYCHIATRIC/SUBSTANCE-RELATED DISORDER, CHILD AND ADOLESCENT

I. Criteria for Admission

All conditions must be met for severity of need and intensity of service to satisfy the criteria for admission.

Severity of Need

Criteria A, B, C, and D must be met to satisfy the criteria for severity of need.

A. The child has a primary DSM-IV diagnosis of an emotional/psychiatric disturbance, significant behavioral problem, and/or a substance use disorder which is the cause of significant functional and psychosocial impairment, and the child's clinical condition can be expected to be stabilized through the provision of medically necessary supervised residential services in a supportive home environment in conjunction with medically necessary treatment, rehabilitation, and support.

B. The child or adolescent requires supervision and active support to ensure the adequate, effective coping skills necessary to live safely in the community, participate in self-care and treatment, and manage the effects of his/her illness. The child's or adolescent's family or caregivers demonstrate an inability to adequately care for the child's or adolescent's physical, emotional, psychosocial, and/or supervision needs. As a result of the child's or adolescent's behavioral problems and/or functional deficits and the family's inability to provide adequate care and supervision of the child or adolescent to ensure his/her safety, there continues to be a risk of one of the following:

1. Hospitalization or other inpatient care as evidenced by the current course of the disorder or by the past history of the disorder; or
2. Harm to self or others as a result of mental illness as evidenced by the current behavior or by the past history.

C. The child's or adolescent's home environment, family resources, and support network are not adequate to provide the level of residential support and supervision currently needed by the child.

D. The child or adolescent is judged to be able to reliably cooperate with the rules and supervision provided and can be safe in a supervised residence.

Intensity of Service

Criteria A and B must be met to satisfy the criteria for intensity of service.

A. Supervised living for children and adolescents will provide supervision and support in a residence outside of the child's or adolescent's own home and provide needed resources and support not sufficiently available within the child's or adolescent's own existing social support system. Clinical intervention services, including behavioral, psychological, and psychosocial therapeutic interventions, may also be provided within supervised residential settings, in lieu of or in addition to outpatient and other community-based mental health services.

B. At least one responsible staff person must be present or available by telephone at all times when there are clients on the premises.

II. Continued Stay Criteria

Criteria A, B, and C must be met to satisfy the criteria for continued stay.

A. The child or adolescent continues to have significant functional impairment as a result of a mental illness and the problems that caused the admission persist to the degree that continued placement in a supervised residence is necessary.
B. The child's or adolescent's family or caregivers continue to demonstrate an inability to adequately care for the child's or adolescent's physical, emotional, psychosocial, and/or supervision needs and, as a result, there continues to be a risk of one of the following:
    1. Inpatient admission; or
    2. Harm to self or others.
C. There is evidence that the resources and social support system which are available to the child or adolescent outside the supervised residence continue to be inadequate to provide the level of residential support and supervision currently needed for safety, care, or effective treatment despite current treatment, rehabilitation, and discharge/disposition planning.

PARTIAL HOSPITALIZATION, PSYCHIATRIC, ADULT

I. Criteria for Admission

All conditions must be met for severity of need and intensity of service to satisfy the criteria for admission.

Severity of Need

Criteria A, B, C, and D must be met to satisfy the criteria for severity of need.

A. Patient must have a diagnosed or suspected mental illness. Mental illness is defined as a psychiatric disorder that, by accepted medical standards, can be expected to improve significantly through medically necessary and appropriate therapy. Presence of the illness(es) must be documented through the assignment of appropriate DSM-IV codes on all applicable axes (I-V).
B. There is clinical evidence that documents that a less intensive outpatient setting is not appropriate at this time and/or a partial hospitalization program can safely substitute for, or shorten, a hospital stay.
C. Either:
    1. There is clinical evidence that the patient would be at risk to self or others if he/she were not in a partial hospitalization program; or

2. As a result of the patient's mental disorder there is an inability to adequately care for one's physical needs, representing potential serious harm to self.
   D. Additionally, either:
   1. The patient can reliably plan for safety in a structured environment under clinical supervision for part of the day and has a suitable environment for the rest of the time; or
   2. The patient is believed to be capable of controlling this behavior and/or seeking professional assistance or other support when not in the partial hospitalization setting.

Intensity of Service

Criteria A, B, C, and D must be met to satisfy the criteria for intensity of service.

A. In order for a partial hospitalization program to be safe and therapeutic for an individual patient, professional and/or social supports must be identified and available to the patient outside of program hours, and the patient must be capable of seeking them as needed.
B. The patient's condition must require a structured program with nursing and medical supervision, intervention, and/or treatment for at least four hours per day.
C. The individualized plan of treatment for partial hospitalization requires treatment by a multidisciplinary team. A specific treatment goal of this team is improving symptoms and level of functioning enough to return the patient to a lesser level of care.
D. A discharge plan is initially formulated that is directly linked to the behaviors and/or symptoms that resulted in admission. This plan receives regular review and revision that includes as appropriate and timely evaluation of post-partial hospitalization needs.

II. Criteria for Continued Stay

Criteria A, B, C, and D must be met to satisfy the criteria for continued stay.

A. All admission criteria are met on a continuing basis.
B. Clinical evidence indicates the persistence of the problems that necessitated the admission to the partial hospitalization program, despite treatment efforts, or the emergence of additional problems consistent with the admission criteria. There should be progress notes for each day that the patient is in a partial hospitalization/day treatment program, docu-

menting the provider's treatment and the patient's response to treatment.
C. The patient's progress confirms that the presenting or newly defined problem(s) will respond to the current treatment plan.
D. Clinical evidence indicates that attempts at therapeutic reentry into a less intensive level of care have resulted or would result in exacerbation of the psychiatric illness to the degree that would warrant the continued need for partial hospitalization services.

PARTIAL HOSPITALIZATION, PSYCHIATRIC, CHILD AND ADOLESCENT

I. Criteria for Admission

All conditions must be met for severity of need and intensity of service to satisfy the criteria for admission.

Severity of Need

Criteria A, B, C, and D must be met to satisfy the criteria for severity of need.

A. Patient must have a diagnosed or suspected mental illness. Mental illness is defined as a psychiatric disorder that, by accepted medical standards, can be expected to improve significantly through medically necessary and appropriate therapy. Presence of the illness(es) must be documented through the assignment of appropriate DSM-IV codes on all applicable axes (I-V).
B. There is clinical evidence that documents that a less intensive outpatient setting is not appropriate at this time and/or a partial hospitalization program can safely substitute for, or shorten, a hospital stay.
C. Either:
   1. There is clinical evidence that the patient would be at risk to self or others if he/she were not in a partial hospitalization program; or
   2. As a result of the patient's mental disorder there is an inability to adequately care for his/her physical needs, representing potential serious harm to self.
D. Additionally, either:
   1. The patient can reliably plan for safety in a structured environment under clinical supervision for part of the day and has a suitable environment for the rest of the time; or

2. The patient is believed to be capable of controlling this behavior and/or seeking professional assistance or other support when not in the partial hospitalization setting.

Intensity of Service

Criteria A, B, C, D, and E must be met to satisfy the criteria for intensity of service.

A. In order for a partial hospitalization program to be safe and therapeutic for an individual patient, professional and/or social supports must be identified and available to the patient outside of program hours, and the patient must be capable of seeking them as needed.
B. The patient's condition must require a structured program with nursing and medical supervision, intervention, and/or treatment for at least four hours per day.
C. The individualized plan of treatment for partial hospitalization requires treatment by a multidisciplinary team. A specific treatment goal of this team is improving symptoms and level of functioning enough to return the patient to a lesser level of care.
D. A discharge plan is initially formulated that is directly linked to the behaviors and/or symptoms that resulted in admission. This plan receives regular review and revision that includes an appropriate and timely evaluation of post-partial hospitalization needs.
E. Patients must receive family therapy a minimum of once per week, unless a specific clinical reason is given as to why this is not needed and is documented in the medical record.

II. Criteria for Continued Stay

Criteria A, B, C, and D must be met to satisfy the criteria for continued stay.

A. All admission criteria are met on a continuing basis.
B. Clinical evidence indicates the persistence of the problems that necessitated the admission to the partial hospitalization program, despite treatment efforts, or the emergence of additional problems consistent with the admission criteria. There should be progress notes for each day that the patient is in a partial hospitalization/day treatment program, documenting the provider's treatment and the patient's response to treatment.
C. The patient's progress confirms that the presenting or newly defined problem(s) will respond to the current treatment plan.

D. Clinical evidence indicates that attempts at therapeutic reentry into a less intensive level of care have resulted or would result in exacerbation of the psychiatric illness to the degree that would warrant the continued need for partial hospitalization services.

PARTIAL HOSPITALIZATION, SUBSTANCE-RELATED DISORDER, ADULT

I. Criteria for Admission

All conditions must be met for severity of need and intensity of service to satisfy the criteria for admission.

Severity of Need

Criteria A, B, and C must be met to satisfy the criteria for severity of need.

A. The provider must be able to document that the individual has a history of alcohol/substance-related disorder meeting DSM-IV criteria but is mentally competent and cognitively stable enough to benefit from admission to a partial hospitalization/day treatment program.
B. The individual requires more intensive multidisciplinary evaluation, treatment, and support than can be provided in a traditional outpatient visit setting or an intensive outpatient program.
C. For individuals with a history of repeated relapses and a treatment history involving multiple treatment attempts, there must be documentation of the restorative potential for the proposed admission.

Intensity of Service

Criteria A, B, C, and D must be met to satisfy the criteria for intensity of service.

A. In order for a partial hospitalization/day treatment program to be safe and therapeutic for an individual patient, professional and/or social supports must be identified and available to the patient outside of program hours, and the patient must be capable of seeking them as needed.
B. The patient's condition must require a structured program with nursing and medical supervision, intervention, and/or treatment for part of each program day.

C. The individualized plan of treatment for partial hospitalization requires treatment by a multidisciplinary team. A specific treatment goal of this team is reduction in severity of symptoms and improvement in level of functioning sufficient to return the patient to a less intensive level of care.

D. A discharge plan is initially formulated that is directly linked to the behaviors and/or symptoms that resulted in admission. This plan receives regular review and revision that includes an appropriate and timely evaluation of post-partial hospitalization needs.

II. Criteria for Continued Stay

Criteria A, B, C, and D must be met to satisfy the criteria for continued stay.

A. All admission criteria are met on a continuing basis.

B. Clinical evidence of the persistence of the problem that caused the admission to partial hospitalization/day treatment, despite therapeutic efforts, or the emergence of additional problems consistent with the partial hospitalization admission criteria that would necessitate continued treatment at this level of care. There should be progress notes written for each treatment day by the provider documenting the provider's treatment and the patient's response to treatment.

C. The patient's progress confirms that the presenting or newly defined problem(s) will respond to the current treatment plan.

D. Clinical evidence indicates that attempts at therapeutic reentry into a less intensive level of care have resulted or would result in relapse or exacerbation of the illness to the degree that would warrant the continued need for intensive treatment services.

PARTIAL HOSPITALIZATION, SUBSTANCE-RELATED DISORDER, CHILD AND ADOLESCENT

I. Criteria for Admission

All conditions must be met for severity of need and intensity of service to satisfy the criteria for admission.

Severity of Need

Criteria A, B, and C must be met to satisfy the criteria for severity of need.

A. The provider must be able to document that the individual has a history of alcohol/substance-related disorder meeting DSM-IV criteria but is mentally competent and cognitively stable enough to benefit from admission to a partial hospitalization/day treatment program.
B. The individual requires more intensive multidisciplinary evaluation, treatment, and support than can be provided in a traditional outpatient visit setting or an intensive outpatient program.
C. For individuals with a history of repeated relapses and a treatment history involving multiple treatment attempts, there must be documentation of the restorative potential for the proposed admission.

Intensity of Service

Criteria A, B, C, D, and E must be met to satisfy the criteria for intensity of service.

A. In order for a partial hospitalization/day treatment program to be safe and therapeutic for an individual patient, professional and/or social supports must be identified and available to the patient outside of program hours, and the patient must be capable of seeking them as needed.
B. The patient's condition must require a structured program with nursing and medical supervision, intervention, and/or treatment for part of each program day.
C. The individualized plan of treatment for partial hospitalization requires treatment by a multidisciplinary team. A specific treatment goal of this team is reduction in severity of symptoms and improvement in level of functioning sufficient to return the patient to a less intensive level of care.
D. A discharge plan is initially formulated that is directly linked to the behaviors and/or symptoms that resulted in admission. This plan receives regular review and revision that includes an appropriate and timely evaluation of post-partial hospitalization needs.
E. Patients must receive intensive family involvement a minimum of once per week, unless a specific clinical reason is given as to why this is not needed and is documented in the medical record.

II. Criteria for Continued Stay

Criteria A, B, C, and D must be met to satisfy the criteria for continued stay.

A. All admission criteria are met on a continuing basis.
B. Clinical evidence of the persistence of the problem that caused the admission to partial hospitalization/day treatment, despite therapeutic ef-

forts, or the emergence of additional problems consistent with the partial hospitalization admission criteria that would necessitate continued treatment at this level of care. There should be progress notes written for each treatment day by the provider documenting the provider's treatment and the patient's response to treatment.

C. The patient's progress confirms that the presenting or newly defined problem(s) will respond to the current treatment plan.

D. Clinical evidence indicates that attempts at therapeutic reentry into a less intensive level of care have resulted or would result in relapse or exacerbation of the illness to the degree that would warrant the continued need for intensive treatment services.

TWENTY-THREE-HOUR BED, PSYCHIATRIC, ADULT

I. Criteria for Admission

All conditions must be met for severity of need and intensity of service to satisfy the criteria for admission.

Severity of Need

Criteria A and B and either C, D, or E must be met to satisfy the criteria for severity of need.

A. Patient must have a diagnosed or suspected mental illness. Mental illness is defined as a psychiatric disorder that, by accepted medical standards, can be expected to improve significantly through medically necessary and appropriate therapy. Presence of the illness(es) must be documented through the assignment of appropriate DSM-IV codes on all applicable axes (I-V).

B. There is a reasonable expectation, based on history, circumstances, or other clearly definable factors, that the patient's disturbance can be sufficiently assessed and palliated in a twenty-three-hour period so as to effect a transfer to a lower level of care.

C. Patient demonstrates imminent risk for severe self-injury, with an inability to guarantee safety, as manifested by any one of the following:

1. Recent, serious, and dangerous suicide attempt, indicated by degree of lethal intent, impulsivity, and/or concurrent intoxication, including an inability to plan reliably for safety.

2. Current suicidal ideation with intent, realistic plan, or available means that is severe and dangerous.

3. Recent self-mutilation that is dangerous and severely compromises the patient's medical and/or functional status.
4. Inability to adequately care for own physical needs, through disordered, disorganized, or bizarre behavior, representing potential for imminent serious harm to self.

D. Patient demonstrates imminent risk for severe injury to others as manifested by any of the following:
1. Active plan, means, and lethal intent to seriously injure others.
2. Recent assaultive behaviors that indicate a high risk for recurrent and serious injury to others.
3. Recent and serious physically destructive acts that indicate a high risk for recurrence and serious injury to others.

E. The patient requires an acute psychiatric intervention(s) that will result in a high probability of serious, imminent, and dangerous deterioration of general medical and/or mental health.

Intensity of Service

Criteria A, B, C, and D must be met to satisfy the criteria for intensity of service.

A. The gathering of a thorough psychiatric and medical assessment by licensed personnel, including a psychiatric evaluation performed by a licensed psychiatrist, sufficient to reach a decision regarding the needed level of care within twenty-three hours.

B. The provision of a physical exam conducted by a licensed physician.

C. The availability of intensive psychiatric and nursing interventions throughout the entire twenty-three hours, including the ability to administer needed medications and, if necessary, suicidal/homicidal observation, quiet room, seclusion, and/or intermittent restraints.

D. The formulation of a plan for continued psychiatric treatment that is in place prior to discharge from the twenty-three-hour setting.

II. Criteria for Continued Stay

Authorization for twenty-three-hour adult psychiatric bed services is not extended beyond the twenty-three-hour period following initiation of the treatment services. It is expected that a disposition will have been made during the twenty-three-hour period as noted above.

INTENSIVE OUTPATIENT TREATMENT,
PSYCHIATRIC, ADULT

I. Criteria for Admission

All conditions must be met for severity of need and intensity of service to satisfy the criteria for admission.

Severity of Need

Criteria A, B, and C must be met to satisfy the criteria for severity of need.

A. The clinical evaluation indicates that the individual has a primary DSM-IV diagnosis or severe emotional disturbance that is the cause of significant psychological, personal care, vocational, educational, and/or social impairment. The individual's disorder can be expected to improve significantly through medically necessary and appropriate therapy. The individual is sufficiently competent, and behaviorally and cognitively stable, to benefit from admission to an intensive outpatient treatment program.

B. The impairment results in at least one of the following:
   1. A clear, current threat to the individual's ability to live in his/her customary setting for an individual who, without that setting and the supports of that setting, would then meet the criteria for a higher level of care, e.g., inpatient or supervised residential care.
   2. A clear, current threat to the individual's ability to be employed or attend school.
   3. An emerging/impending risk to the safety or property of the individual or of others.

C. Either:
   1. For individuals with persistent or recurrent disorders, the individual's past history indicates that when the patient has experienced similar clinical circumstances, less intensive treatment was not sufficient to prevent clinical deterioration, stabilize the disorder, support effective rehabilitation, or avert the need for a more intensive level of care due to increasing risks to the patient or others; or
   2. For individuals with an acute disorder, crisis, or those transitioning from an inpatient to a community setting, there is clinical evidence that less intensive treatment will not be sufficient to prevent clinical deterioration, stabilize the disorder, support effective rehabilitation,

or avert the need to initiate or continue a more intensive level of care due to current risk to the patient or others.

Intensity of Service

Criteria A, B, and C must be met to satisfy the criteria for intensity of service.

A. In order for intensive outpatient services to be safe and therapeutic for an individual, professional and/or social supports must be identified and available to the individual outside of program hours, and the individual must be capable of seeking them as needed when not attending the program.
B. The individual's condition must require an integrated program of rehabilitation counseling, education, therapeutic, and/or family services at least two hours/day or for six hours in a week.
C. The individual treatment plan for intensive outpatient services requires that the services are provided by a multidisciplinary team of professional and supervised support staff. A specific treatment goal of the treatment team is reduction in severity of symptoms and improvement in level of functioning sufficient to return the patient to outpatient treatment follow-up and/or self-help support groups.

II. Criteria for Continued Stay

Criteria A, B, C, and D must be met to satisfy the criteria for continued stay.

A. All admission criteria are met on a continuing basis.
B. Clinical evidence indicates the persistence of the problems that necessitated the admission to the intensive outpatient treatment program, despite treatment efforts, or the emergence of additional problems consistent with the admission criteria. There should be progress notes for each day that the patient is in an intensive outpatient treatment program, documenting the provider's treatment and the patient's response to treatment.
C. The patient's progress confirms that the presenting or newly defined problem(s) will respond to the current treatment plan.
D. Clinical evidence indicates that attempts at therapeutic reentry into a less intensive level of care have resulted or would result in exacerbation of the psychiatric illness to the degree that would warrant the continued need for intensive outpatient treatment services.

INTENSIVE OUTPATIENT TREATMENT, PSYCHIATRIC, CHILD AND ADOLESCENT

I. Criteria for Admission

All conditions must be met for severity of need and intensity of service to satisfy the criteria for admission.

Severity of Need

Criteria A, B, and C must be met to satisfy the criteria for severity of need.

A. The clinical evaluation indicates that the individual has a primary DSM-IV diagnosis or severe emotional disturbance that is the cause of significant psychological, personal care, vocational, educational, and/or social impairment. The individual's disorder can be expected to improve significantly through medically necessary and appropriate therapy. The individual is sufficiently competent, and behaviorally and cognitively stable, to benefit from admission to an intensive outpatient treatment program.

B. The impairment results in at least one of the following:
   1. A clear, current threat to the individual's ability to live in his/her customary setting for an individual who, without that setting and the supports of that setting, would then meet the criteria for a higher level of care, e.g., inpatient or supervised residential care.
   2. A clear, current threat to the individual's ability to be employed or attend school.
   3. An emerging/impending risk to the safety or property of the individual or of others.

C. Either:
   1. For individuals with persistent or recurrent disorders, the individual's past history indicates that when the patient has experienced similar clinical circumstances, less intensive treatment was not sufficient to prevent clinical deterioration, stabilize the disorder, support effective rehabilitation, or avert the need for a more intensive level of care due to increasing risks to the patient or others; or
   2. For individuals with an acute disorder, crisis, or those transitioning from an inpatient to a community setting, there is clinical evidence that less intensive treatment will not be sufficient to prevent clinical deterioration, stabilize the disorder, support effective rehabilitation, or avert the need to initiate or continue a more intensive level of care due to current risk to the patient or others.

Intensity of Service

Criteria A, B, C, and D must be met to satisfy the criteria for intensity of service.

A. In order for intensive outpatient services to be safe and therapeutic for an individual, professional and/or social supports must be identified and available to the individual outside of program hours, and the individual must be capable of seeking them as needed when not attending the program.
B. The individual's condition must require an integrated program of rehabilitation counseling, education, therapeutic, and/or family services at least two hours/day or for six hours in a week.
C. The individual treatment plan for intensive outpatient services requires that the services are provided by a multidisciplinary team of professional and supervised support staff. A specific treatment goal of the treatment team is reduction in severity of symptoms and improvement in level of functioning sufficient to return the patient to outpatient treatment follow-up and/or self-help support groups.
D. Patient cases must demonstrate family involvement in therapy at least once a week, unless a specific clinical reason is given as to why this is not needed and is documented in the medical record.

II. Criteria for Continued Stay

Criteria A, B, C, and D must be met to satisfy the criteria for continued stay.

A. All admission criteria are met on a continuing basis.
B. Clinical evidence indicates the persistence of the problems that necessitated the admission to the intensive outpatient program, despite treatment efforts, or the emergence of additional problems consistent with the admission criteria. There should be progress notes for each day that the patient is in an intensive outpatient treatment program, documenting the provider's treatment and the patient's response to treatment.
C. The patient's progress confirms that the presenting or newly defined problem(s) will respond to the current treatment plan.
D. Clinical evidence indicates that attempts at therapeutic reentry into a less intensive level of care have resulted or would result in exacerbation of the psychiatric illness to the degree that would warrant the continued need for intensive outpatient services.

INTENSIVE OUTPATIENT TREATMENT, SUBSTANCE-RELATED DISORDER, ADULT

I. Criteria for Admission

All conditions must be met for severity of need and intensity of service to satisfy the criteria for admission.

Severity of Need

Criteria A, B, and C must be met to satisfy the criteria for severity of need.

A. The clinical evaluation indicates that the individual has a primary diagnosis(es) of substance abuse/dependence meeting DSM-IV criteria and is sufficiently mentally competent and cognitively stable to benefit from admission to an intensive outpatient program.
B. Individual requires more intensive treatment and support than can be provided in a traditional outpatient visit setting, i.e., needs to be involved in treatment three or more times per week for two or more hours per session. The patient's condition reflects a pattern of severe alcohol and/or drug use as evidenced by periods of inability to maintain abstinence over a consistent period of time.
C. For individuals with a history of repeated relapses and a treatment history involving multiple treatment attempts in intensive outpatient or partial hospitalization programs, there must be documentation of the restorative potential for the proposed program admission.

Intensity of Service

Criteria A, B, and C must be met to satisfy the criteria for intensity of service.

A. In order for intensive outpatient services to be safe and therapeutic for an individual, professional and/or social supports must be identified and available to the individual outside of program hours, and the individual must be capable of seeking them as needed when not attending the program.
B. The individual's condition must require an integrated program of rehabilitation counseling, education, therapeutic, and/or family services at least two hours/day or for six hours in a week.
C. The individual treatment plan for intensive outpatient services requires that the services are provided by a multidisciplinary team of profes-

sional and supervised support staff. A specific treatment goal of the treatment team is reduction in severity of symptoms and improvement in level of functioning sufficient to return the patient to outpatient treatment follow-up and/or self-help support groups.

II. Criteria for Continued Stay

Criteria A, B, C, and D must be met to satisfy the criteria for continued stay.

A. All admission criteria are met on a continuing basis.
B. Clinical evidence indicates the persistence of the problems that necessitated the admission to the intensive outpatient program, despite treatment efforts, or the emergence of additional problems consistent with the admission criteria. There should be progress notes for each day that the patient is in an intensive outpatient treatment program, documenting the provider's treatment and the patient's response to treatment.
C. The patient's progress confirms that the presenting or newly defined problem(s) will respond to the current treatment plan.
D. Clinical evidence indicates that attempts at therapeutic reentry into a less intensive level of care have resulted or would result in exacerbation of the psychiatric illness to the degree that would warrant the continued need for intensive outpatient services.

INTENSIVE OUTPATIENT TREATMENT, SUBSTANCE-RELATED DISORDER, CHILD AND ADOLESCENT

I. Criteria for Admission

All conditions must be met for severity of need and intensity of service to satisfy the criteria for admission.

Severity of Need

Criteria A, B, and C must be met to satisfy the criteria for severity of need.

A. The clinical evaluation indicates that the individual has a primary diagnosis(es) of substance abuse/dependence meeting DSM-IV criteria and is sufficiently mentally competent and cognitively stable to benefit from admission to an intensive outpatient program.

B. Individual requires more intensive treatment and support than can be provided in a traditional outpatient visit setting, i.e., needs to be involved in treatment three or more times per week for two or more hours per session. The patient's condition reflects a pattern of severe alcohol and/or drug use as evidenced by periods of inability to maintain abstinence over a consistent period of time.
C. For individuals with a history of repeated relapses and a treatment history involving multiple treatment attempts in intensive outpatient or partial hospitalization programs, there must be documentation of the restorative potential for the proposed program admission.

Intensity of Service

Criteria A, B, C, and D must be met to satisfy the criteria for intensity of service.

A. In order for intensive outpatient services to be safe and therapeutic for an individual, professional and/or social supports must be identified and available to the individual outside of program hours, and the individual must be capable of seeking them as needed when not attending the program.
B. The individual's condition must require an integrated program of rehabilitation counseling, education, therapeutic, and/or family services at least two hours/day or for six hours in a week.
C. The individual treatment plan for intensive outpatient services requires that the services are provided by a multidisciplinary team of professional and supervised support staff. A specific treatment goal of the treatment team is reduction in severity of symptoms and improvement in level of functioning sufficient to return the patient to outpatient treatment follow-up and/or self-help support groups.
D. Patients must receive family therapy a minimum of once per week, unless a specific clinical reason is given as to why this is not needed and is documented in the medical record.

II. Criteria for Continued Stay

Criteria A, B, C, and D must be met to satisfy the criteria for continued stay.

A. All admission criteria are met on a continuing basis.
B. Clinical evidence indicates the persistence of the problems that necessitated the admission to the intensive outpatient program, despite treatment efforts, or the emergence of additional problems consistent with the ad-

mission criteria. There should be progress notes for each day that the patient is in an intensive outpatient treatment program, documenting the provider's treatment and the patient's response to treatment.

C. The patient's progress confirms that the presenting or newly defined problem(s) will respond to the current treatment plan.

D. Clinical evidence indicates that attempts at therapeutic reentry into a less intensive level of care have resulted or would result in exacerbation of the psychiatric illness to the degree that would warrant the continued need for intensive outpatient services.

OUTPATIENT TREATMENT, PSYCHIATRIC AND SUBSTANCE- RELATED DISORDER

I. Criteria for Initial Treatment Report Review

All conditions must be met for severity of need and intensity of service to satisfy the criteria for the initial treatment report review.

Severity of Need

Criteria A, B, C, and D must be met to satisfy the criteria for severity of need.

A. A DSM-IV diagnosis on Axis I and/or Axis II.

B. Completed assessments on Axes III, IV, and V.

C. A description of DSM-IV psychiatric symptoms, intrapsychic conflict, behavioral and/or cognitive dysfunction consistent with the diagnoses on Axes I and II.

D. Either 1, 2, or 3 below must be met to satisfy criterion D:

1. At least mild symptomatic distress and/or impairment in functioning due to psychiatric symptoms and/or behavior in at least one of the three spheres of functioning (occupational, scholastic, or social) that are the direct result of an Axis I or Axis II disorder. This is evidenced by specific clinical description of the symptom(s) and/or impairment(s) consistent with a GAS (DSM-IV Axis V) score of less than 71.

2. The individual has a persistent DSM-IV illness for which maintenance treatment is required to maintain optimal symptom relief and/or functioning.

3. There is clinical evidence that further therapy is required to support termination of therapy, although the individual no longer has at least mild symptomatic distress or impairment in functioning. The factors considered in making a determination about the continued medical

necessity of treatment in this termination phase are the frequency and severity of previous relapse, level of current stressors, and other relevant clinical indicators. The therapist should be able to explain whether the treatment being utilized will change (and if not, why) when there has been sustained improvement as measured in part by a GAS score over 70.

Intensity of Service

Criteria A and B must be met to satisfy the criteria for intensity of service.

A. A medically necessary and appropriate treatment report, or its update, specific to the patient's impairment in functioning and DSM-IV psychiatric symptoms, behavior, cognitive dysfunctions, and/or psycho dynamic conflicts. The treatment plan is expected to be effective in either:
1. Alleviating the patient's distress and/or dysfunction; or
2. Achieving appropriate maintenance goals for a persistent illness; or
3. Supporting termination.
B. The treatment report must identify 1 through 6 to satisfy criterion B:
1. The status of target-specific DSM-IV psychiatric symptoms, behavior, and cognitive dysfunction being treated.
2. The current, or anticipated modifications in, biologic, behavioral, psychodynamic, or psychosocial framework(s) of treatment for each psychiatric symptom/cluster and/or behavior.
3. The status of specific and measurable goals for treatment specified in terms of symptom alleviation, behavioral change, cognitive alteration, psychodynamic change, or improvement in social, occupational, or scholastic functioning.
4. The current, or anticipated modifications in, treatment methods in terms of:
a. treatment framework or orientation
b. treatment modality
c. treatment frequency
d. estimate of treatment duration
5. Status of measurable, target criteria used to identify both interim treatment goals and end of treatment goals (unless this is a maintenance treatment) to substantiate that (a) treatment is progressing, and/or (b) goals have been met and treatment is no longer needed.
6. An alternative plan to be implemented if the patient does not make substantial progress toward the given goals in a specified period of

time. Examples of an alternative plan are a second opinion or introduction of adjunctive or alternative therapies.

II. Criteria for Continued Treatment

Criteria A, B, C, and D must be met to satisfy the criteria for continued outpatient treatment.

A. The intensity of service criteria for the initial treatment report review continue to be met.
B. A DSM-IV diagnosis on Axis I and/or a personality disorder diagnosis on Axis II.
C. A description of DSM-IV psychiatric symptoms, intrapsychic conflict, cognitive dysfunction, or behavior consistent with the diagnoses given.
D. Either 1, 2, or 3 must be met to satisfy criterion D:
   1. There is the persistence or recurrence of at least mild symptomatic distress and/or impairment in functioning due to these psychiatric symptoms and/or behavior.
   2. The individual has a persistent DSM-IV illness for which maintenance treatment is required to maintain optimal symptom relief and/or functioning.
   3. There is clinical evidence that further therapy is required to support termination of therapy, although the individual no longer has at least mild symptomatic distress or impairment in functioning. The factors considered in making a determination about the continued medical necessity of treatment in this termination phase are the frequency and severity of previous relapse, level of current stressors, and other relevant clinical indicators. The therapist should be able to explain whether the treatment being utilized will change (and if not, why) when there has been sustained improvement as measured in part by a GAS score over 70.

NURSING HOME CONSULTATIVE TREATMENT, PSYCHIATRIC AND SUBSTANCE-RELATED DISORDER

I. Criteria for the Initial Treatment Report Review

All conditions must be met for severity of need and intensity of service to satisfy the criteria for the initial treatment report review.

Severity of Need

Criteria A, B, C, and D must be met to satisfy the criteria for severity of need.

A. A DSM-IV diagnosis on Axis I and/or Axis II.
B. Completed assessments on Axes III, IV, and V.
C. A description of DSM-IV psychiatric symptoms, intrapsychic conflict, behavioral and/or cognitive dysfunction consistent with the diagnoses on Axes I and II.
D. Either 1, 2, or 3 below must be met to satisfy criterion D:
    1. At least mild symptomatic distress and/or impairment in functioning due to psychiatric symptoms and/or behavior in at least one of the three spheres of functioning (occupational, scholastic, or social) that are the direct result of an Axis I or Axis II disorder. This is evidenced by specific clinical description of the symptom(s) and/or impairment(s) consistent with a GAS (DSM-IV Axis V) score of less than 71. Symptoms and behaviors are not solely deterioration in cognitive functioning or an inability to care for activities of daily living resulting from a dementia.
    2. The individual has a persistent DSM-IV illness for which maintenance treatment is required to maintain optimal symptom relief and/or functioning.
    3. There is clinical evidence that further therapy is required to support termination of therapy, although the individual no longer has at least mild symptomatic distress or impairment in functioning. The factors considered in making a determination about the continued medical necessity of treatment in this termination phase are the frequency and severity of previous relapse, level of current stressors, and other relevant clinical indicators. The therapist should be able to explain whether the treatment being utilized will change (and if not, why) when there has been sustained improvement as measured in part by a GAS score over 70.

Intensity of Service

Criteria A and B must be met to satisfy the criteria for intensity of service.

A. A medically necessary and appropriate treatment report, or its update, specific to the patient's impairment in functioning and DSM-IV psychiatric symptoms, behavior, cognitive dysfunctions, and/or psychodynamic conflicts. Treatment is not offered solely as a substitute for socialization or related activities. The treatment report is expected to be effective in either:

1. Alleviating the patient's distress and/or dysfunction; or
2. Achieving appropriate maintenance goals for a persistent illness; or
3. Supporting termination.

B. The treatment report must identify 1 through 6 to satisfy criterion B:

1. The status of target-specific DSM-IV psychiatric symptoms, behavior, and cognitive dysfunction being treated.
2. The current, or anticipated modifications in, biologic, behavioral, psychodynamic, or psychosocial framework(s) of treatment for each psychiatric symptom/cluster and/or behavior.
3. The status of specific and measurable goals for treatment specified in terms of symptom alleviation, behavioral change, cognitive alteration, psychodynamic change, or improvement in social, occupational, or scholastic functioning.
4. The current, or anticipated modifications in, treatment methods in terms of:
   a. treatment framework or orientation
   b. treatment modality
   c. treatment frequency
   d. estimate of treatment duration
5. Status of measurable, target criteria used to identify both interim treatment goals and end of treatment goals (unless this is a maintenance treatment) to substantiate that (a) treatment is progressing; and/or (b) goals have been met and treatment is no longer needed.
6. An alternative plan to be implemented if the patient does not make substantial progress toward the given goals in a specified period of time. Examples of an alternative plan are a second opinion or introduction of adjunctive or alternative therapies.

II. Criteria for Continued Treatment

Criteria A, B, C, and D must be met to satisfy the criteria for continued outpatient treatment.

A. The intensity of service criteria for the initial treatment report review continue to be met.
B. A DSM-IV diagnosis on Axis I and/or a personality disorder diagnosis on Axis II.
C. A description of DSM-IV psychiatric symptoms, intrapsychic conflict, cognitive dysfunction, or behavior consistent with the diagnoses given.

D. Either 1, 2, or 3 must be met to satisfy criterion D:

1. There is the persistence or recurrence of at least mild symptomatic distress and/or impairment in functioning due to these psychiatric symptoms and/or behavior.
2. The individual has a persistent DSM-IV illness for which maintenance treatment is required to maintain optimal symptom relief and/or functioning.
3. There is clinical evidence that further therapy is required to support termination of therapy, although the individual no longer has at least mild symptomatic distress or impairment in functioning. The factors considered in making a determination about the continued medical necessity of treatment in this termination phase are the frequency and severity of previous relapse, level of current stressors, and other relevant clinical indicators. The therapist should be able to explain whether the treatment being utilized will change (and if not, why) when there has been sustained improvement as measured in part by a GAS score over 70.

THERAPEUTIC LEAVE OF ABSENCE DOCUMENTATION

Therapeutic leave of absence (TLOA) is any leave from a facility which is ordered by a physician, medically necessary, and not supervised by staff. A leave for medical reasons (e.g., consultations, evaluations, office visits, and treatments) is excluded from this definition.

Documentation Guidelines

To ensure that a TLOA is recognized as meeting the above definition, the medical record must contain the following information:

1. A physician must order each TLOA, identify it as a TLOA, and specify the number of leave hours approved.
2. Therapeutic rationale must be included in the ITPs, and/or physician progress notes, and/or social worker notes.
3. The nurse, physician, or social worker must document the outcome of the TLOA in the medical record.

Medical Necessity

While these guidelines address the documentation of therapeutic leaves of absence, the medical necessity of each leave of absence continues to be determined by the application of the psychiatric hospitalization criteria.

NOTES

1. It is recognized that life-threatening intoxication/poisoning (i.e., endangering vital functions—central nervous system, cardiac, respiratory) may need acute medical attention but that attention is generally not considered detoxification. In such cases, general medical/surgical criteria generally are applied instead of these criteria for detoxification.

2. For patients who present with both serious biomedical and substance abuse/dependency illnesses, it is necessary that medical/surgical and behavioral health specialists comanage the care. In most instances, these patients' care is most optimally provided in medical/surgical facilities with behavioral health care provided as consultation.

Bibliography

Chapter 1

Bond, J.T., Galinsky, E., and Swanberg, J.E. (1998). *The National Study of the Changing Workplace*. New York: Families and Work Institute.

Cagney, T. (1998). Defining the Profession: EAPA and Health Care-Managed Care Laws. *EAPA Exchange*, 28(2): 10-11.

EAPA (1997). *1997 Member Resources Directory*. Arlington, VA: EAPA.

MacDonald, S.B. (1998) Clarifying the EAP-Health Care Law Connection. *EAPA Exchange*, 28(2): 12-15.

Masi, D.A. (1998). *The Role of Employee Assistance Programs in Managed Behavioral Healthcare*. Rockville, MD: Department of Health and Human Services, Public Health Services, Substance Abuse and Mental Health Services Administration.

Narrow, W., Regier, D., and Rae, D. (1993). Use of Services by Persons with Mental and Addictive Disorders. *Archives of General Psychiatry*, 50: 95-107.

Oss, M.E. and Clary, J. (1998). EAPs Are Evolving to Meet Changing Employer Needs. *Open Minds*, 12(1): 4-10.

Strosahl, K. (1994). New Dimensions in Behavioral Health/Primary Care Integration. *HMO Practice*, 8: 176-179.

Turner, S. and Davis, S. (2000). EAPs and Work/Life Programs: Solutions to the Whole Puzzle. *EAPA Exchange*, 30(5): 21-23.

U.S. Department of Health and Human Services (DHHS) (1993). *Depression in Primary Care: Detection, Diagnosis and Treatment*. Rockville, MD: U.S. Department of Health and Human Services, Public Health Service, Agency for Health Care Policy and Research.

U.S. Department of Health and Human Services (DHHS). (1999). *Mental Health: A Report of the Surgeon General*. Rockville, MD: U.S. Department of Health and Human Services, Substance Abuse and Mental Health Administration, Center for Mental Health Services, National Institutes of Health, National Institute of Mental Health.

Von Korff, M. and Simon, G. (1996). The Prevalence and Impact of Psychological Disorders in Primary Care: HMO Research Needed to Improve Care. *HMO Practice*, 10(December): 150-165.

Winegar, N.D. (1996). *The Clinician's Guide to Managed Behavioral Care*. Binghamton, NY: The Haworth Press.

Chapter 2

Blakely, S. (1998). The Backlash Against Managed Care. *Nations Business,* July 16-24.
Mazzarella, D. (1998). Immune from Suits, HMOs Crimp Fearlessly on Care. Editorial. *USA Today,* July 15, p. 10A.

Chapter 3

American Psychiatric Association (1994). *Diagnostic and Statistical Manual of Mental Disorders,* Fourth Edition. Washington, DC: American Psychiatric Association.
Bento, R.F. (1997) On the Other Hand . . . The Paradoxical Nature of Employee Assistance Programs. *Employee Assistance Quarterly,* 13(2): 83-91.
Employee Assistance Program Management Letter (1998). 11(12): 1-2.
Hufnagel, P. (1998). The Long and Worthwhile Road to EA Licensure. *EAPA Exchange, 28(2): 38-39.*
McKibbon, D. (1998). Governance of the CEAP: The EACC. *EAPA Exchange,* 28(2): 35.

Chapter 4

Employee Assistance Association, Houston Chapter (1996). *Ethical Dilemmas in Workplace Counseling: A Casebook.* Houston, TX: EAPA.
Hass, L.J. and Malouf, J.L. (1995). *Keeping Up the Good Work: A Practitioner's Guide to Mental Health Ethics.* Sarasota, FL: Professional Resource Press.
Haynes, J. and Singleton, J. (1993). *The Professional's Guide to Drug and Alcohol Testing.* Knoxville, TN: AlcoPro.
NHCAA (2001). Estimated Financial Loss to Fraud Fact Sheet. <www.nhcaaorg/factsheet_impact_loss.htm> accessed February 19, 2001.
Tarasoff v. Regents of the University of California (1976). 551 P. 2d 334.

Chapter 5

Gee, Y. (1999). The role of the union steward in the EAP process. *EAPA Exchange,* 29(4): 14.
Kotler, P. (1986). *The Principles of Marketing,* Third Edition. Englewood Cliffs, NJ: Prentice-Hall.
Lawson, T.E. (2000). Making a business case for employee assistance. *EAP Digest,* 20(2): 18-22.
Masi, D. (1994). *Evaluating Your Employee Assistance and Managed Behavioral Care Program.* Troy, MI: Performance Press.

Chapter 6

U.S. Department of Health and Human Services (U.S. DHHS) (1999). *Mental Health: A Report of the Surgeon General.* Rockville, MD: U.S. Department of Health and Human Services.

Index

Managed care organization (MCO), 21,
27-35
definition of, 27
directory of companies, 89
EAP clients and, 45-49
managing managed care process,
48-49
MBHO care referrals, 49-54
role and responsibilities, 45-47
understanding coverage, 47-48
innovations in, 75-87
psychopharmacology
management services, 75-80
use of internet, 80-87
investigation of health care fraud,
62-64
key functions, 31-35
outpatient precertification, 31,
32-35
roles of MBHO care managers, 32
origins of, 30
referral, 39
strategies, 27-30
consumer incentives, 27
discounted reimbursement rates,
27-29
exclusion, 29
group practices, 28
PCP gatekeeping, 29
utilization review, 29
Management, of people, 24
Marketing and selling, of EAPs, 65-73
determining key decision makers
in purchase, 70-73
professional meeting attendance
by decision makers, 72-73
targeting advertising, 72
developing customer success stories,
67-70
employer stories, 68
end user stories, 68-69
tracking and communicating,
69-70
sample sales proposal, 91-105
commitment to accreditation, 92
conclusion, 105

Marketing and selling, of EAPs, sample
sales proposal *(continued)*
EAP product overview, 92-105
product offerings, 91-92
understanding target market, 66-67
Masi, Dale, 7-12
MBHO. *See* Managed care organization
(MCO)
MCO. *See* Managed care organization
(MCO)
Medical necessity, definition, 108
MyDailyHealth, 84-87

National Health Care Anti-Fraud
Association (NHCAA), 62
National Study of the Changing
Workforce (NSCW), 15-21
implications for employee assistance
professionals, 20-21
key findings, 16-20
child and elder care duties
and obligations, 18-19
demographics of the workplace,
16-17
employer-sponsored benefits
for child and elder care
assistance, 19
family life facts, 17-18
job satisfaction and commitment
to employers, 20
opinions about jobs, 19-20
NHCAA, 62
Nonclinical services, 8-9
NSCW. *See* National Study of the
Changing Workforce
(NSCW)
Nursing home consultative treatment,
156-159

OAP, 6
Occupational alcoholism program
(OAP), 6